Invitation to MEDITERRANEAN COOKING

Invitation to
MEDITERRANEAN
COOKING

150 Vegetarian and Seafood Recipes

CLAUDIA RODEN

Photography by
GUS FILGATE

RIZZOLI
NEW YORK

For my children, Simon, Nadia and Anna, and for Ros and Clive, who have joined the family—with my thanks for eating through the book with me.

First published in the United States of America in 1997 by
RIZZOLI INTERNATIONAL PUBLICATIONS, INC.
300 Park Avenue South, New York, NY 10010

First published in Great Britain in 1997 by
Pavilion Books Limited
26 Upper Ground, London SE1 9PD

Text © 1997 Claudia Roden
Photographs © 1997 Gus Filgate

Library of Congress Cataloging-in-Publication Data

Roden, Claudia.
        Invitation to Mediterranean cooking / Claudia Roden.
                p.   cm.
        Includes index.
        ISBN 0-8478-2020-3 (hardcover)
        1. Cookery, Mediterranean. I. Title
TX725.M35R627   1997
641.59' 1822—dc21   97-10536
                                                        CIP

Home Economist for photography: Maxine Clark
Stylist: Penny Markham
Designer: Janet James
Front cover: Eggs Baked with Peppers and Tomatoes (page 119)
Back cover: Ricotta Cake (page 212)

Color reproduction by D.P. Reprographics
Printed and bound in Spain by Graficas Reunidas, S.A. (Madrid)

CONTENTS

INTRODUCTION

THE MEDITERRANEAN DIET—
A MODEL OF HEALTHY EATING

In the late 1960s the world became aware of the work of the American nutritionist Ancel Keys, who studied the link between diet and disease in seven countries and found that almost all the countries around the Mediterranean had a lower rate of cardiovascular diseases, cancer, and various other chronic diseases. His discoveries triggered a flood of research in all corners of the world. Some countries, such as Italy and Finland, changed the diets of entire villages and noted the results. Immigrant communities whose eating habits changed in new homelands were also studied.

Although there are bound to be contradictions in any nutritional theory, the results of these studies showed that despite other factors such as genetics, lifestyle, and environment, diet was the obvious major cause of disease. The so-called Western diseases of affluence were linked to diets low in fiber and high in sugar and saturated animal fats. A diet rich in grains, vegetables, fruits, and nuts, with plenty of fish and little meat, using oil as the main cooking fat, was determined to be helpful in reducing the instances of disease.

A worldwide consensus gradually emerged. The World Health Organization, the Food and Agricultural Organization, and all the major world health reports have come up with the same recommendations: eat more wheat, rice, beans, lentils, chick peas, and nuts, lots of fresh vegetables and fruit, more fish, less red meat, and cook with oil rather than butter. Many governments have issued food guidelines based on these recommendations.

Olive oil, in particular, has been heralded as an effective weapon in the fight against disease. Since time immemorial, it has been believed to have curative and nutritive properties—a panacea for all kinds of illnesses, and modern science has confirmed its beneficial qualities. It is high in monounsaturated fats and fatty acids and rich in vitamin E, which is an antioxidant that is believed to help prevent heart and lung diseases and cancer. Like all vegetable and seed oils, it is cholesterol-free. And it has the added effect of reducing so-called 'bad' cholesterol (low-density lipoproteins) and increasing 'good' cholesterol (high-density lipoproteins).

Of course, other parts of the world where people use large quantities of oil, vegetables, fruits, and pulses could have been used as a model for healthy eating, but the Mediterranean style has been adopted as the best way to encourage people to change their eating habits because of its very special appeal. Mediterranean food is flavorful, aromatic, and colorful. This corner of the world is immensely seductive, with its blue sea and sky, magical light and scented air, fairs, street markets, and open-air terraces. The people of the Mediterranean have mastered an art of casual, leisurely, healthy living that we would all do well to emulate.

A CULINARY RENAISSANCE

For years, in restaurants and hotels around the Mediterranean, local cooking had been overshadowed by French classic cuisine. When tourism was born at the end of the nineteenth century and high society discovered the Côte d'Azur, the luxury hotels and restaurants adopted the grand style of French gastronomy, which became the model to which the Mediterranean and the world aspired.

In more recent times, the move from countryside to towns, the mass-production of food, the arrival of convenience and fast-foods, and mass tourism have all contributed to the loss of traditional regional cooking. A French sociologist remarked cynically that *la cuisine du terroir* (the regional cooking of the land) exists only in cookery books. But it is not quite so. Nostalgia for a vanishing heritage and the fear of losing cultural identity, as well as a general change of tastes and values, have resulted in a revival of interest in regional, rustic cuisines in France and the rest of the Mediterranean region.

The top French chefs in Provence and the Côte d'Azur who went through their nouvelle cuisine rebellion against 'mummified Parisian classicism,' have now turned to regional produce and styles for inspiration. In Italy, where *piatti tipici*, as they call local regional dishes, began to appear on restaurant menus little more than a decade ago, professional cooks say they want to update and revitalize the old dishes, not embalm them. They call the trend *il recupero* and *la riscoperta*. In every country around the Mediterranean, including Turkey, Egypt, Morocco, and Tunisia, restaurants that had once been ashamed to offer anything but foreign classics are now proud to serve their own local dishes.

Another phenomenon is the way Mediterranean foods, especially the rustic, country, and 'poor' foods, have become fashionable all over the world and now are considered representative of modern cooking. Star chefs in Britain and America are inspired by the produce and styles of the Mediterranean, and supermarkets stock all the necessary ingredients. It is especially gratifying to see how healthy eating and the pleasures of the table have converged.

In the beginning interest was focused primarily on the cooking of southern Italy and Provence but more recently it has spread to all the varied cuisines of the area, in particular to the more exotic eastern and southern Mediterranean.

THE CHARM OF THE MEDITERRANEAN

Although Mediterranean dishes are extraordinarily varied and there are many cooking styles in the sixteen or so countries around the little inland sea, there is a certain unity throughout the Mediterranean basin, which means that if you know one cuisine, you will be able to understand the others, and many of the dishes can be seen as variations on a theme.

The unity has to do with the sharing of climate and produce, with the intense traffic and trading activity between the port cities, and with an incestuous history.

Since ancient times, settlers, colonizers, and empires spread out across the area, introducing new produce, utensils, and methods, and leaving their mark everywhere. The first wave of colonists—the Phoenecians, Greeks, and Romans—established the trinity of wheat, olives, and vines. The Arabs, who were the dominant force beginning in the seventh century (they occupied part of Spain for 700 years and Sicily for 200), established new trading systems and spread the cultivation of foods such as rice, sugarcane, apricots, and oranges (bitter oranges and lemons were known to the Romans), pomegranates, dates, bananas, artichokes, spinach, and eggplants. Other important influences were the kingdom of Catalunya, which conquered Sicily, Sardinia, and Naples and penetrated the south of France; and the crown of Aragon, which had possessions around the Mediterranean. The Normans and the Republic of Venice, which had colonies as far away as Alexandria, also introduced their cooking styles to the Mediterranean shores. One of the greatest unifying forces was the Ottoman Empire, which lasted for 500 years until its collapse at the end of World War I. It spread a style of cooking, drawn from its conquered territories, to all the nations in the empire.

Apart from empires and colonists, movements of populations contributed to an interchange of cooking styles: the Moors returned to North Africa after their expulsion from Spain, Tunisians moved to Palermo to build the cathedral, Sicilian peasants were brought to Algeria by the French colonists to work the land, troubadours and jongleurs from southern France were seen in Italy and Catalonia, and spice merchants and itinerant traders were seen everywhere. More recently, the French *pieds noirs*, resettling in the south of France, and immigrant workers from North Africa, have had an enormous impact.

A surprisingly unified culinary culture was woven from these disparate threads: Andalusia, Provence, and southern Italy have more in common with their maritime neighbors than with the northern regions of their own countries. Throughout the Mediterranean cooks use the same clay pots, the same wood-burning ovens, mortars and pestles, skewers, and grills. You find similar dishes: cooked vegetables preserved in olive oil and eaten cold, stuffed vegetables, fluffy vegetable omelettes, rice dishes, creamy puddings, almond pastries, and tomato sauce, the signature of Mediterranean cuisine.

There are, of course, also many differences that distinguish one country's cuisine from that of another. Where the French use cognac, Sicilians use Marsala and Spaniards use sherry. Where Italians use Pecorino Romano or ricotta, the French use Gruyère or goat cheese and the Greeks and Turks use feta. While a fish soup in the French Midi is flavored with orange peel and saffron, in Italy it is flavored with white wine, hot peppers, and parsley, and in Tunisia with cumin, paprika, cayenne, and cilantro. Parsley, cilantro, and mint are favorite herbs in the eastern Mediterranean, while basil and marjoram are favorites in the western part. A western Mediterranean dish may use vanilla and grated orange zest, in place of the eastern Mediterranean orange-flower or rose water and cinnamon. Egyptians mix fried garlic with crushed coriander seeds, and Turks combine cinnamon with allspice. The olive tree has a strong historical and cultural association with the Mediterranean, and the juice pressed from olives is the traditional cooking oil of the region; although not all the countries use it exclusively, it is certainly used liberally, as is lemon juice, and most recipes call for garlic, though usually not in very large amounts and always in a way that softens the flavor; herbs and spices add a beguiling touch to Mediterranean dishes. Combine this with the visual appeal of ingredients like peppers, tomatoes, pumpkin, and black olives, and you get something quite enchanting.

From the wealth of dishes of the area, I have picked only personal favorites. My goal was not to cover all of the countries, to feature famous dishes, or to include an example of every type of food. It was to offer fresh, light, delicious, casual food for every day, and quick and easy to cook, as well as some more elaborate dishes that are ideal for entertaining and special occasions and are fun to serve. The dishes are naturally in line with the ideals of healthy eating, but the pleasures of cooking and eating are the main focus of this book.

Although there are no meat dishes in the book, the aim is to appeal to meat-eaters who wish to vary and extend their diet, as well as to vegetarians. Meat was never featured largely in Mediterranean cooking: meat was very highly prized, but the peasantry could rarely afford it. In some countries it was eaten only once a week or only on festive occasions. In Christian countries, the medieval Church forbad meat on Fridays and during Lent, so for almost a third of the year, fish and legumes took the place of meat. Fish was prepared simply, but a great deal of inventiveness and ingenuity went into creating vegetable dishes. Luckily, the area was blessed with a propitious climate and soil, and provided a wide variety of vegetables, nuts, and fruit. That is why the Mediterranean is an Eden for vegetarians.

Tips from a Mediterranean Kitchen
Planning a Vegetarian Meal

The book has been organized in short chapters to make it easy to select a vegetarian menu. Each chapter, except Vegetable Side Dishes, Desserts, and Basics, contains recipes for good main dishes. A light summer meal can consist of a salad or two served with good bread, accompanied, if you like, with cheese, while a simple winter meal can be soup with bread. A family meal may be one dish such as a pasta, risotto, or cracked wheat pilaf, an egg dish, cheese bake, tart, flan, or gratin, served with a salad and followed by fresh fruit.

For a small dinner party, have a soup or appetizer to start, and follow with cheese and dessert. Dishes such as vegetable couscous can be served as a one-dish meal. For a grander affair for many people, you may like to serve a variety of appetizers and main dishes, which can be made in advance and reheated if necessary.

The Mediterranean way is to end with fresh fruit, but I have included many desserts because guests look forward to a sweet dessert at dinner parties. Most of the desserts in this book are made with fruits that celebrate the produce of the Mediterranean.

PLANNING A FISH OR SEAFOOD MEAL

A fish soup accompanied by toasted bread can be a meal in itself, followed by a fruit or a dessert. Or you can plan around a seafood pasta, couscous, or fish flan. The most common Mediterranean way is to grill, broil, or fry fish as simply as possible. A marinade or dressing is the usual embellishment and there are sauces to accompany. You can start the meal with a vegetable soup or appetizer or with seafood such as shrimp, scallops, or mussels. Serve the fish with a salad or with one of the vegetable, rice, or cracked wheat side dishes.

ABOUT THE INGREDIENTS

Eggs: Throughout the book, large eggs are used.

Tomatoes: The taste of the tomatoes we get at our greengrocers and supermarkets has greatly improved in the last few years, but it still does not compare to the intense flavor of the brilliant red plum tomatoes and the huge curvy, indented tomatoes that have ripened in the Mediterranean sun. As the quality varies from shop to shop, it is difficult to specify one type of tomato as the best to choose. At my local supermarket the plum tomatoes are the tastiest and that is what I generally use for most dishes.

Flat-leaf parsley: The parsley of the Mediterranean region is the flat-leaf variety, which has a different flavor than our curly parsley. But curly parsley may be substituted if flat-leaf parsley is unavailable.

Olives: Olives are a symbol of the Mediterranean. They all ripen from green and yellow, through red and violet, to purple and black. Cured and preserved black and green olives are served as appetizers and for breakfast, to accompany bread and cheese, and are used in many dishes. There are many excellent varieties: every Mediterranean country produces some very good ones. The fleshy Greek Kalamata, the Spanish Manzanilla, the small black Taggiasca from Liguria, and large green Cerignola of Puglia in Italy are famous, as are the sweet black wrinkled olives of Provence and the tiny ones of Nice. Unfortunately, all the varieties that are sold pitted are invariably tasteless, so for recipes that require pitted or chopped olives you will have to stone them yourself.

Olive Oil: With the extraordinary range of fine extra virgin olive oils available now from different countries, and the growing snobbery and mystique that surrounds this newly fashionable product, it is good to explore the qualities of the different oils for yourself. Like everything else in matters of taste, the best olive oil is the one you like best. And since one olive oil may be good in one context while a different one is good in another, it is worth experimenting.

Oils vary in color, flavor, and aroma, depending on the type of tree, the soil in which it grows, whether it grows on a hill or the plain or by the sea, the weather, when and how the olives are harvested, how ripe they are, how quickly the oil is extracted and by what means. The old traditional method is to crush and grind the olives, pits and all, and let the oil rise gradually to the top of the extracted liquid. New methods of production now most commonly used, called 'continuous' methods, separate the liquid from the solid paste, then the oil from the rest of the juice by spinning the paste or liquid at high speed in a drum or centrifuge. The extra virgin oils produced from first cold pressings by either of these methods are the finest, with the richest flavor and aroma. The bottled varieties can be varietal oils (from a single type of olive) or blends. The blending of oils of two or more varieties of different origin with complementary characteristics is an art that usually entails mixing neutral oils with strong-tasting ones to produce a perfect balance. The oils produced by single estates are the most prestigious and expensive, but some of the extra virgin oils produced more cheaply by large commercial operators can be wonderful too. Unfortunately, however, many of these are lacking in the desirable qualities, and many of the very expensive oils are hardly worth the price.

Oils can be light and delicate, or assertive and strong, and their flavors and aromas simple or complex. Flavors range from sweet to pleasantly bitter, fruity, nutty, spicy, and peppery. The flavors can be experienced immediately or as an aftertaste. Fragrance may be fruity, floral, nutty or grassy, elusive or intense. As with wine, some harvests produce exceptional oil, some more ordinary oils. Blended oils are always the same, as blenders seek to achieve consistency by adjusting their mixes. Their styles reflect local tastes and traditions as well as the preferences—for lightness, for instance—of consumers in countries newly introduced to olive oil.

You cannot tell the style or quality of an oil by its color, but a dark green is generally characteristic of a fruity, bitter, astringent oil produced from green olives that have not reached maturity, and golden yellow oils made from sweet ripe black olives late in the season (all olives start green and ripen to black). However, it is not uncommon for green leaves to be crushed with the olives to give color to the oil.

In general, the best oils of Provence are light, sweet, and fragrant; the oils of Greece are slightly bitter, assertive, and hearty; Portuguese oils are rough and rustic. Spain produces a variety of fruity, aromatic oils—Catalan oils have a delicious almond quality while Andalusian oils have a warm, sweet fruit taste and heady perfume. Italy is famous for the strongly assertive, bitter quality of its Tuscan oils whose peppery aftertaste grates the back of the throat, but the lesser known light, sweet, fruity oils from Liguria, Umbria, and the Abruzzi, and the rich, fruity, peppery ones of Apulia, are also very appealing. While all

Mediterranean countries produce a certain amount of olive oil, Tunisia and Turkey, where every bit of the countryside is dotted with olive trees, are important producers whose oils are not easily available in Europe. They do not benefit from EC subsidies and cannot afford to promote themselves. Much of the Tunisian product goes to Italy and some to Spain and France to be blended and re-exported. Some of the Italian blends also use Greek and Spanish oils.

Different types of oil are suitable for different dishes. There are no fixed rules, and tastes vary. The best extra virgin oils should be used raw, as a dressing. I like a light, fresh, nonastringent, fragrant oil to dress salads, fish, and boiled vegetables, and to blend into delicate raw sauces; and a rich, fruity oil for gazpachos and herby green sauces, to dress pasta and drizzle over broiled or fried vegetables, meat, or fish. A drop of strong-tasting, bitter, fruity or spicy oil will enhance the taste of a creamy soup, a stew, or a tomato sauce, and makes a rich dressing for pasta. For deep-frying, use oils labeled ordinary virgin olive oil, refined olive oil, or simply olive oil. These are produced from second or subsequent pressings, which have then been processed and refined to remove their acidity, and are usually bland.

Some people like to flavor their oil with aromatics such as garlic cloves, chilies, bay leaves, fennel seeds, sprigs of basil, rosemary, or thyme. These should be left in the oil for two weeks, then removed, as they may rot.

Harissa: A fiery hot pepper and garlic paste with spices from North Africa can be bought from Middle Eastern stores. It is best bought in a tube rather than in a can, as you need only a little at a time. To make it yourself, see page 219.

Pepper: Black pepper, preferably freshly ground, is used throughout the book, unless otherwise stated.

Pomegranate syrup: This is the concentrated syrup or molasses of boiled and reduced sour pomegranate juice. It is available in Middle Eastern stores.

Drinks: The traditional spirit of the Mediterranean is flavored with aniseed—in France it is pastis, distilled from grapes; in the Middle East it is called arak, raki, ouzo, or zibib; and in Morocco it is mahia, made from figs or dates. They are always served with appetizers. Beer and whisky are other warm-weather drinks. In Muslim countries the usual refreshments are pressed lemon, fresh fruit juices, iced syrups, and yoghurt beaten with iced water or soda.

In non-Muslim countries wine is always served with meals. It is a habit worth adopting. A simple and robust wine with character and quality, which can stand up to an amalgam of flavors, is what you need. Vinegar and lemon will turn a thin, dry wine flat, and sweetness will make it acid, while spices and chilies will kill a great and complex wine. A young, vigorous wine with rough fruit goes well with sour, sweet, spicy, and savory flavors. With a fruity dessert you can serve a sweet wine.

Strong black coffee—Turkish or espresso—is the perfect ending to an authentic Mediterranean meal.

ABOUT MEASURES

I have sometimes given numbers of vegetables as well as the weight, only as a rough guide. Bear in mind that sizes vary considerably from one greengrocer and supermarket to another, let alone from one country to another, and that what is considered medium or large also varies (I have found, for instance, that in different stores between 5 to 8 'medium' tomatoes weighed 1 pound).

The baking dishes I have used are generally round clay ones, but square and rectangular ones will do just as well. The size given is the diameter. I have also used round cake pans.

People in the Mediterranean are not overly concerned with precise measures and prefer to judge by eye if a dish is the right size. They also rely on their taste for such things as adjusting seasonings and aromatics. I would like to encourage you to do the same and trust your good sense, because that really never fails, even if you are dealing with a dish that is new to you.

SALADS AND APPETIZERS

Salads and cold vegetable dishes, served as appetizers with drinks, or as side dishes, are some of the most appealing features of Mediterranean eating. They enliven a meal with their traditionally strong flavourings (spices and aromatics are meant to sharpen the appetite) and exuberant colours, and bring variety and excitement to the table. One advantage is that they can be prepared in advance. You can also make a meal out of two or three appetizers accompanied with bread, and perhaps cheese and olives.

1 BUNCH (2 OUNCES) ARUGULA LEAVES

3 MEDIUM TOMATOES, QUARTERED

3 TABLESPOONS LIGHT EXTRA VIRGIN OLIVE OIL

JUICE OF 1/2 LEMON

SALT AND PEPPER

ABOUT 6 SCALLIONS, SLICED

ARUGULA AND TOMATO SALAD

This is an Egyptian salad.

SERVES 4

Cut the arugula leaves into ribbons. Put them in a bowl with the tomatoes and toss with the remaining ingredients.

MIXTURE OF SALAD LEAVES (ABOUT 7 OUNCES) SUCH AS GEM LETTUCE, OAK LEAVES, CURLY ENDIVE, BELGIAN ENDIVE, WATERCRESS, ARUGULA, LAMB'S LETTUCE (CORN SALAD), DANDELION, AND PURSLANE

1/2 TO 3/4 CUP MIXED CHOPPED FRESH HERBS SUCH AS CHERVIL, BASIL, MARJORAM, CHIVES, MINT, PARSLEY, OR CILANTRO

VINAIGRETTE (SEE PAGE 218)

MIXED GREEN LEAF AND HERB SALAD

This type of salad became famous long ago as the Provençal *mesclun* and now all our supermarkets sell mixed greens inspired by it.

SERVES 4

Put the salad leaves in a wide shallow bowl and sprinkle on the herbs.

Just before serving, dress them lightly with the Vinaigrette.

VARIATIONS

Add fried garlic slices or garlic croutons made by rolling small cubes of bread in olive oil flavored with a little crushed garlic, and toasting them.

Sprinkle with fresh walnut halves.

RIGHT Mixed Green Leaf and Herb Salad

2 BUNCHES (ABOUT 9 OUNCES) PURSLANE

4 PLUM TOMATOES, QUARTERED

2 SMALL OR 1 LARGE CUCUMBER, PEELED AND CUT INTO THICK SLICES

4 SCALLIONS, SLICED

VINAIGRETTE (SEE PAGE 218)

4 OUNCES FETA CHEESE, CUT INTO 3/4-INCH CUBES (OPTIONAL)

8 BLACK OLIVES (OPTIONAL)

PURSLANE SALAD WITH TOMATO AND CUCUMBER

Purslane is one of the Mediterranean salad leaves that has yet to be discovered here. You can find the fleshy leaves occasionally, sold in bunches, in Greek and Middle Eastern stores. You can shred them or leave them whole for this salad, which makes a light meal.

SERVES 4

Pull the purslane leaves off the stems. Put the leaves in a bowl with the rest of the vegetables and dress with the Vinaigrette.

Garnish with feta cheese and olives.

JUICE OF 1/2 ORANGE

JUICE OF 1/2 LEMON

1/2 TABLESPOON ORANGE-FLOWER WATER

2 TABLESPOONS SESAME, HAZELNUT, OR A LIGHT EXTRA VIRGIN OLIVE OIL

SALT

1 HEAD CURLY ENDIVE OR BATAVIA OR 2 SMALL HEADS ROMAINE, CUT INTO RIBBONS

2 LARGE ORANGES (SWEET OR SOUR), PEELED AND SLICED

LETTUCE AND ORANGE SALAD

Oranges are used in a variety of salads in Morocco, where the delicately flavored argan oil is used to dress them. You may wish to try sesame or hazelnut oil.

SERVES 4

Mix together the orange and lemon juices, orange-flower water, oil, and salt. Lightly dress the lettuce and scatter in a wide serving dish.

Lay the orange slices on top.

CHOPPED CUCUMBER AND MINT SALAD

**This Middle Eastern cucumber
salad is delicately scented and refreshing.**

SERVES 4

1 LARGE CUCUMBER, PEELED AND
GRATED OR CHOPPED IN A FOOD
PROCESSOR

3 TABLESPOONS EXTRA VIRGIN
OLIVE OIL

2 TABLESPOONS LEMON JUICE OR 1
TABLESPOON WHITE WINE VINEGAR

ABOUT 1 TABLESPOON ORANGE-
FLOWER WATER

SALT

1 TABLESPOON DRIED CRUSHED
MINT LEAVES

BLACK AND GREEN OLIVES
(OPTIONAL)

Drain the cucumber. Just before serving, mix with the rest of the ingredients. Garnish, if you like, with the olives.

NAVY BEAN SALAD

**This is the famous Turkish *piaz*.
It makes a snack or light meal.**

SERVES 4

2 (14-OUNCE) CANS NAVY OR
CANNELLINI BEANS

5 TABLESPOONS EXTRA VIRGIN
OLIVE OIL

2 TABLESPOONS WHITE WINE
VINEGAR

SALT AND PEPPER

1 MEDIUM MILD ONION, FINELY
CHOPPED

3 TABLESPOONS CHOPPED FLAT-LEAF
PARSLEY

10 BLACK OLIVES

2 FIRM BUT RIPE TOMATOES, CUT
INTO WEDGES

2 HARD-BOILED EGGS, CUT INTO
WEDGES

Drain the beans, dress with oil, vinegar, salt and pepper to taste, and mix with the chopped onion and parsley.

Serve garnished with olives, tomatoes, and hard-boiled eggs.

*OVERLEAF From left to right:
Lettuce and Orange Salad (page 18)
and Moroccan Zucchini Purée
(page 26)*

2 FENNEL BULBS

VINAIGRETTE (SEE PAGE 218)

FENNEL SALAD

The delicate anise flavor of fennel is particularly pleasant when it is eaten raw.

SERVES 4

Cut the fennel bulbs into slices vertically. Arrange on a serving plate and pour on the vinaigrette.

2 LARGE CARROTS, CHOPPED OR GRATED IN THE FOOD PROCESSOR

3 TABLESPOONS PEANUT OR LIGHT VEGETABLE OIL

1 CLOVE GARLIC, CRUSHED

1/2 TEASPOON CINNAMON

SALT

2 TO 3 TABLESPOONS LEMON JUICE

1/2 CUP PLAIN OR THICK, STRAINED GREEK YOGHURT

MOROCCAN CARROT SALAD WITH YOGHURT

This surprisingly soft, creamy salad will do well as an appetizer or side dish.

SERVES 4

Sauté the carrots in the oil with the garlic over low heat, stirring often, for about 10 minutes, until slightly softened but not colored. Add the cinnamon, salt, and lemon juice and cook for about 5 more minutes. Set aside to cool to room temperature then chill in the refrigerator.

Serve the salad cold on a plate with the yoghurt poured on top.

RIGHT Fennel Salad

4 LARGE CARROTS, PEELED

2 CLOVES GARLIC, CRUSHED

1 TO 2 TABLESPOONS WHITE WINE VINEGAR

4 TABLESPOONS EXTRA VIRGIN OLIVE OIL

1/2 TEASPOON GROUND CUMIN

6 BLACK OR GREEN OLIVES

1 PRESERVED LEMON PEEL (SEE PAGE 219), CUT INTO SMALL PIECES (OPTIONAL)

SPICY CARROT PURÉE

Many North African appetizers are strongly flavored, usually with cumin, which is meant to whet the appetite.

SERVES 4

Boil the carrots in water until they are soft. Drain and mash them with a fork. Add the garlic, vinegar, oil, and cumin and mix well. Serve cold, garnished with olives and Preserved Lemon Peel.

2 LARGE CARROTS, CUT INTO 3/4-INCH SLICES

1 LARGE SWEET POTATO, CUT INTO 3/4-INCH CUBES

4 TABLESPOONS SEEDLESS RAISINS OR SULTANAS

1/2 TEASPOON POWDERED GINGER

1/2 TEASPOON CINNAMON

SALT AND PEPPER

3 TABLESPOONS EXTRA VIRGIN OLIVE OIL

1 TABLESPOON HONEY

JUICE OF 1/2 LEMON

CARROT AND SWEET POTATO SALAD

This North African appetizer is sweet and delicate.

SERVES 4

Put the carrots and sweet potatoes in a pan with enough water to cover. Stir in the rest of the ingredients and simmer, uncovered, for about 15 minutes, or until the carrots and sweet potatoes are tender, and the sauce is syrupy and thick.

Set aside to cool to room temperature then chill in the refrigerator. Serve cold with its sauce.

1 CUP LARGE BROWN OR GREEN
LENTILS, SOAKED FOR 1 HOUR

SALT

1 MEDIUM ONION, CHOPPED

5 TO 6 TABLESPOONS EXTRA VIRGIN
OLIVE OIL

1 TEASPOON GROUND CORIANDER

11 OUNCES FRESH SPINACH

JUICE OF 1/2 TO 1 LEMON

PEPPER

VARIATIONS

Use frozen leaf spinach.
Defrost and add to the
fried onion. Sprinkle with
salt and cook, stirring, for
5 to 8 minutes.

Use chick peas or navy
beans (canned if you like)
instead of the lentils.

For a different lentil salad
with tomato and cheese,
mix the cooked lentils with
3 medium diced ripe
tomatoes and 4 ounces
crumbled feta cheese and
dress with Vinaigrette (see
page 218).

LENTIL AND
SPINACH SALAD

**Spinach is paired with every one of the
Mediterranean legumes—chick peas, beans, split peas,
and lentils—in soups, stews, and salads.
It is one of the age-old combinations that works well.
This salad is an old Arab favorite, often
accompanied by yoghurt.**

SERVES 4

Drain the lentils and simmer in fresh water for 20
minutes or until tender, adding a pinch of salt toward the
end, then drain.

In a large pan over medium heat, fry the onion in
2 tablespoons of the oil until soft. Stir in the ground
coriander and turn the heat to low.

Meanwhile, wash the spinach and remove the
stems only if they are tough. Drain, press all the water
out, and put into the pan with the onion. Sprinkle lightly
with salt, cover with a lid, and let the leaves steam for
about 1 minute, or until they crumple into a soft mass.

Add the lentils, lemon juice, pepper to taste, and
the remaining oil, and mix well. Remove from the heat,
let cool to room temperature, and serve.

ABOUT 3 LARGE ZUCCHINI

1 TO 2 CLOVES GARLIC, CRUSHED

JUICE OF $^1/_2$ LEMON

3 TABLESPOONS EXTRA VIRGIN
OLIVE OIL

$^1/_2$ TEASPOON GROUND CUMIN

SALT

PINCH OF CHILI POWDER

4 OUNCES FETA CHEESE, CRUMBLED
WITH A FORK (OPTIONAL)

6 GREEN AND BLACK OLIVES
(OPTIONAL)

MOROCCAN ZUCCHINI PURÉE

SERVES 4

Boil the zucchini in water until soft. Drain and mash with a fork. Add the garlic, lemon juice, oil, cumin, salt to taste, and chili powder, and stir well.

Garnish with feta cheese and olives, if you like.

OLIVE OR VEGETABLE OIL FOR FRYING

ABOUT 3 LARGE ZUCCHINI, CUT INTO SLICES LENGTHWISE

SALT

1 3/4 CUPS PLAIN OR STRAINED GREEK YOGHURT, AT ROOM TEMPERATURE

FRIED ZUCCHINI SLICES WITH YOGHURT

For this traditional Arab way of serving zucchini, the vegetables may be broiled rather than deep-fried.

SERVES 4

Heat the oil to 350°F. Deep-fry the zucchini until they are lightly browned, turning them over once, then drain them on paper towels and sprinkle with salt.

Alternatively, broil them. Arrange the zucchini slices on a baking sheet. Brush both sides very lightly with olive oil and sprinkle with salt. Put the baking sheet under the broiler, and cook, turning the slices over once, until browned.

Serve hot or at room temperature with yoghurt poured over.

VARIATIONS

The yoghurt may be flavored with 1 crushed garlic clove and 2 teaspoons dried crumbled mint. The yoghurt should be at room temperature, even when the zucchini are served hot.

Another traditional accompaniment is tomato sauce (see page 218).

Eggplant may be prepared in the same way. Before frying, the eggplant slices are usually salted and left to degorge their juices for 30 minutes.

1 POUND BABY EGGPLANTS

SALT

5 CLOVES GARLIC, PEELED

4 TABLESPOONS EXTRA VIRGIN OLIVE OIL

2 TABLESPOONS POMEGRANATE SYRUP

JUICE OF 1/2 LEMON

1/4 TEASPOON CHILI PEPPER

1/2 TEASPOON CUMIN

3 TABLESPOONS CHOPPED FLAT-LEAF PARSLEY

MARINATED BABY EGGPLANTS

You find baby eggplants, which are about 4 inches long, in Indian and Middle Eastern stores. The dish keeps well for several days.

SERVES 4 TO 6

Wash the eggplants, remove the caps but leave the stems. Cut in half lengthwise, not right to the end, so that the halves remain attached at the stem end.

Boil in salted water with the garlic cloves for 15 minutes, then drain.

For the marinade, mash the boiled garlic cloves and mix with the rest of the ingredients. Roll the drained eggplants in the marinade, opening them so that the cut sides can absorb it well. Leave for at least half a day and serve at room temperature.

1 LARGE EGGPLANT

2 TABLESPOONS POMEGRANATE SYRUP

3 TABLESPOONS EXTRA VIRGIN OLIVE OIL

SALT AND PEPPER TO TASTE

1 TO 2 CLOVES GARLIC, CRUSHED (OPTIONAL)

2 TABLESPOONS CHOPPED FLAT-LEAF PARSLEY

EGGPLANT PURÉE WITH POMEGRANATE SYRUP

This is a Syrian version of the famous eggplant caviar (see variation) which is found all over the Mediterranean. The dark, almost black, pomegranate syrup gives it an exciting sweet-and-sour flavor and an intriguing color (the syrup is sold in Middle Eastern stores as pomegranate concentrate or molasses). Accompany with warm bread for dipping.

SERVES 4

VARIATION

For the traditional eggplant caviar, add the juice of ½ to 1 lemon instead of the pomegranate syrup.

Roast and peel the eggplant as described on page 217. Press the juices out in a colander and finely chop the flesh with two pointed knives (this gives a better texture than blending in a food processor). Do the chopping in the colander, letting the juices escape.

Put the chopped eggplant in a bowl, add the rest of the ingredients, and mix well. Spread the purée on a serving dish, sprinkle with parsley, and serve.

2 MEDIUM EGGPLANTS, CUT INTO
SLICES ABOUT ⅓-INCH THICK

SALT

OLIVE OR VEGETABLE OIL FOR
FRYING

2 TO 3 TABLESPOONS
POMEGRANATE SYRUP

3 CLOVES GARLIC, COARSELY
CHOPPED

3 TABLESPOONS CHOPPED FLAT-LEAF
PARSLEY

VARIATIONS

You can omit the
pomegranate syrup and
instead serve the fried
eggplant slices spread with
a layer of thick, strained
yoghurt, or tossed in Fresh
Tomato Sauce (see page
218).

FRIED EGGPLANT SLICES WITH POMEGRANATE SYRUP

**In all Mediterranean countries fried
eggplants are common everyday fare. This
Syrian version, dressed with
pomegranate syrup, is particularly delicious.**

SERVES 4

Sprinkle the eggplant slices generously with salt, and
leave them for 30 minutes to degorge their juices. Rinse
and dry with paper towels.

Deep-fry in about ½-inch of oil. The oil should be
hot at first, then lower the heat a little, so that the slices
do not brown too quickly before they are soft inside. Turn
over once. Drain on paper towels and pat gently with
more towels on top.

Arrange in a serving dish. Mix the pomegranate
syrup with 3 tablespoons water and place a little on each
eggplant slice.

Fry the garlic in 4 tablespoons of the frying oil in a
small pan, until golden.

Sprinkle the eggplant with the fried garlic and the
parsley and serve at room temperature.

2 CLOVES GARLIC, FINELY CHOPPED

2 TABLESPOONS EXTRA VIRGIN
OLIVE OIL

ABOUT 6 MEDIUM RIPE TOMATOES,
PEELED AND CHOPPED

1 TO 2 TEASPOONS SUGAR

SALT

1/2 TEASPOON PAPRIKA (OPTIONAL)

A LARGE PINCH OF CHILI PEPPER
(OPTIONAL)

3 RED AND YELLOW BELL PEPPERS

PEPPER AND TOMATO APPETIZER

This North African appetizer, called *shoucouka*, can be sweet or peppery hot. Serve it with bread.

SERVES 4

Fry the garlic in the oil until golden, then add the tomatoes, sugar, salt, and the paprika and chili if using. Cook over very low heat for 30 minutes or until the sauce is thick and jam-like.

Roast and peel the bell peppers (see page 216). Reserve the roasting juices and add them to the tomato sauce.

Cut the peeled peppers into small squares and stir into the tomato sauce. Remove from the heat and let cool to room temperature. Chill in the refrigerator and serve cold.

1 MEDIUM ONION, CHOPPED

4 TABLESPOONS EXTRA VIRGIN
OLIVE OIL

3 CLOVES GARLIC, CHOPPED

ABOUT 10 SMALL FROZEN
ARTICHOKE HEARTS OR BOTTOMS,
SLICED OR QUARTERED

7 OUNCES SHELLED GREEN PEAS OR
PETITS POIS

7 OUNCES SHELLED FAVA BEANS

2 TABLESPOONS CHOPPED FRESH
MINT

2 TABLESPOONS CHOPPED FRESH
DILL

SALT AND PEPPER

JUICE OF 1/2 LEMON

2 TEASPOONS SUGAR

TIP

*It is sometimes difficult to find
baby artichokes that you can
eat whole and it is a big effort
to trim the usual artichokes to
obtain the hearts. I use frozen
artichoke hearts or bottoms
(canned ones are not much
good). You can now get shelled
fava beans and peas at some
supermarkets. At an Iranian
store near my house where I get
my frozen artichoke bottoms
(from Egypt in 14-ounce packs),
I recently found very good
frozen shelled fava beans.*

BRAISED FAVA BEANS, PEAS, AND ARTICHOKES

**A combination of fava beans and artichokes
is found in almost every Mediterranean
country. In Sicily green peas are added.**

SERVES 4 TO 6

Fry the onion in the oil until golden.

Add the garlic, artichokes, peas, and beans, and
sauté gently, stirring, for about 2 minutes.

Add the mint and dill, salt and pepper to taste,
lemon juice, sugar, and about 4 tablespoons water. Cook,
covered, for 10 minutes or until the vegetables are
tender, adding a little water if necessary.

Serve hot or at room temperature.

NOTE To prepare and use fresh artichoke hearts, see
page 217.

1 POUND SHIITAKE MUSHROOMS OR A MIXTURE OF OTHER VARIETIES

1 MEDIUM ONION, CHOPPED

3 TABLESPOONS EXTRA VIRGIN OLIVE OIL

3 GARLIC CLOVES, CHOPPED

JUICE OF 1/2 LEMON

2/3 CUP FRUITY DRY WHITE WINE

SALT AND PEPPER

3 TABLESPOONS CHOPPED FLAT-LEAF PARSLEY

MUSHROOMS WITH GARLIC AND WHITE WINE

This is a traditional way of cooking mushrooms in France and Italy. A mixture of wild mushrooms including boletus, chanterelles, and morels makes a splendid but very expensive dish. Shiitakes are a very good alternative. Serve them, if you like, with toasted brioche halves or slices.

SERVES 4

Clean the mushrooms and cut very large ones into 1-inch pieces.

Sauté the onion lightly in the oil until soft. Add the mushrooms and garlic and cook until their juices have evaporated.

Add the lemon juice and the wine, season with salt and pepper to taste, and cook for 5 to 10 minutes more, until the mushrooms are cooked through.

Stir in the parsley and serve hot or at room temperature.

1 LARGE ONION, CHOPPED

5 TABLESPOONS EXTRA VIRGIN
OLIVE OIL

1 1/2 POUNDS SWEET POTATOES, CUT
INTO 1 1/2-INCH CUBES

1/2 TO 3/4 TEASPOON POWDERED
GINGER

PINCH GROUND SAFFRON
(OPTIONAL)

1 TEASPOON PAPRIKA

1 TEASPOON CINNAMON

PINCH OF CAYENNE

JUICE OF 1/2 TO 1 LEMON

2 TEASPOONS SUGAR

SALT

4 TABLESPOONS CHOPPED CILANTRO
OR FLAT-LEAF PARSLEY

SWEET POTATO SALAD

**In this Moroccan salad, the curious mix of
sweet and spicy is quite delicious. It is nice as
it is but you may add, if you like, a handful
of black olives, chopped Preserved Lemon Peel (see
page 219), and a tablespoon of capers.**

SERVES 4

In a saucepan, fry the onion in 3 tablespoons of the oil until soft. Add the sweet potatoes and water to just cover.

Stir in the ginger, saffron, if using, paprika, cinnamon, cayenne, lemon juice, sugar, and salt to taste. Cook, uncovered, for 15 minutes or until the sweet potatoes are tender, turning the potatoes over once; be careful not to let them overcook and fall apart.

The sauce should be reduced to a thick, syrupy consistency. If it is not, transfer the potatoes with a slotted spoon to a serving dish and boil the sauce to reduce. At the last minute, stir in the cilantro and the remaining oil. Remove from the heat, let cool to room temperature, and serve.

1 1/2 POUNDS POTATOES

SALT AND PEPPER

4 TABLESPOONS EXTRA VIRGIN
OLIVE OIL

1 1/2 TABLESPOONS WHITE WINE
VINEGAR

1/2 TEASPOON HARISSA (SEE PAGE
219) OR A LARGE PINCH OF
CAYENNE (OPTIONAL)

2 OUNCES ANCHOVY FILLETS,
FINELY CHOPPED (OPTIONAL)

1 TO 3 CLOVES GARLIC, CRUSHED
(OPTIONAL)

1 LARGE BUNCH (ABOUT 1/2 CUP)
PARSLEY, FINELY CHOPPED

2 TABLESPOONS CAPERS, SQUEEZED
TO GET RID OF EXCESS VINEGAR

MASHED POTATO SALAD
WITH ANCHOVIES

**This Tunisian salad can be served
as an appetizer or side salad and goes well
with fish. The anchovies are optional.**

SERVES 4 TO 6

Peel and boil the potatoes in lightly salted water until soft, then drain, reserving a little of the cooking water.

Mash the potatoes with the oil and vinegar and 2 to 4 tablespoons of the cooking water until they have a soft, moist texture. Add the rest of the ingredients and mix well. Serve at room temperature.

1 1/2 CUPS SHELLED WALNUTS

1 1/2 TO 2 TABLESPOONS TOMATO
PASTE

1 SLICE WHOLE WHEAT BREAD,
CRUSTS REMOVED, TOASTED

8 TABLESPOONS EXTRA VIRGIN
OLIVE OIL

2 TABLESPOONS POMEGRANATE
SYRUP OR THE JUICE OF 1/2 LEMON

1 TEASPOON COARSELY GROUND
HOT RED CHILI FLAKES OR A PINCH
OF CHILI POWDER

1 TEASPOON CUMIN

2 TEASPOONS SUGAR

SALT TO TASTE

SPICY WALNUT PASTE

**This delicious Turkish relish, called
muhammara, can be served as a dip with bread
or to accompany a salad. It keeps very well for
several days, so you can make a large batch.
Pomegranate syrup, also called concentrate
or molasses, can be found in Middle Eastern
and sometimes Indian stores.**

SERVES 6 TO 8

Blend everything together to a paste in the food processor.

*RIGHT Spicy Walnut Paste and
Focaccia (page 221)*

³/₄ CUP FINE OR MEDIUM GROUND
BULGHUR

ABOUT 6 MEDIUM TOMATOES,
PEELED AND PURÉED IN A FOOD
PROCESSOR

JUICE OF ¹/₂ LEMON

1 TEASPOON TOMATO PASTE

3 TO 4 TABLESPOONS EXTRA VIRGIN
OLIVE OIL

SALT

CHILI FLAKES OR CHILI POWDER TO
TASTE

1 SMALL MILD ONION OR 5
SCALLIONS, FINELY CHOPPED

²/₃ CUP WALNUTS OR PISTACHIOS,
OR A MIXTURE OF THE TWO

BULGHUR SALAD
WITH WALNUTS

**In this scrumptious and nutritious Turkish
salad, called *batrik*, bulghur is soaked in
the juice of fresh puréed tomatoes and is enriched
with walnuts, pistachios, and onions.
It can be made mild or hot with chili pepper.**

SERVES 4 TO 6

Mix the bulghur with the tomatoes, lemon juice, and
tomato paste and set aside for 1 hour, or until the grain
has absorbed the juice and become tender. Add oil, salt,
and chili flakes to taste. Just before serving, add the
onion and walnuts.

1¹/₄ CUPS MEDIUM COUSCOUS

1 GREEN OR RED BELL PEPPER,
DICED

3 MEDIUM TOMATOES, PEELED
AND DICED

10 SCALLIONS, THINLY SLICED

SALT AND PEPPER TO TASTE

JUICE OF 1 LEMON, OR MORE
TO TASTE

5 TO 8 TABLESPOONS EXTRA VIRGIN
OLIVE OIL

A FEW SPRIGS FRESH MINT,
SHREDDED

1 LARGE BUNCH (¹/₂ CUP) FLAT-
LEAF PARSLEY, CHOPPED

COUSCOUS SALAD

**I have not come across a couscous salad
in North Africa, but France is awash
with what they call *taboulé* (the name of the
Lebanese bulghur, mint, and parsley salad).**

SERVES 4 TO 6

Put the couscous in a bowl, cover with 1¹/₄ cups cold
water, and mix well. Set aside to soak for at least 30
minutes. When the grain is swollen and tender, stir in
the rest of the ingredients.

RIGHT Bulghur Salad with Walnuts

2 LARGE ONIONS

1/2 CUP LIGHT EXTRA VIRGIN OLIVE OIL

3/4 CUP LARGE BROWN LENTILS, SOAKED IN COLD WATER FOR 1 HOUR

1/2 TEASPOON CINNAMON

1/2 TEASPOON ALLSPICE

3/4 CUP LONG-GRAIN OR BASMATI RICE

SALT AND PEPPER

VARIATION

Another method, which might be easier, is to boil the lentils and the rice in separate pots, then drain and mix together when each is done.

BROWN LENTILS AND RICE WITH CARAMELIZED ONIONS

In Syria and Lebanon this classic dish is called *mudardara*. In Egypt, it is known as *megadarra*. It is eaten cold or warm, usually accompanied with yoghurt and a cucumber and tomato salad. American long-grain rice does not need to be washed but basmati rice does. Pour boiling water over it, stir and leave for a few minutes, then rinse in cold water in a sieve.

SERVES 4 TO 6

Slice 1½ onions into half moons and sauté in 3 tablespoons of the oil, over medium heat, stirring frequently, until they are very dark brown and almost caramelized. Set aside.

Chop the remaining onion and fry in 1 tablespoon of the oil over medium heat until soft and golden.

Drain and simmer the lentils in 3 cups water with the cinnamon and allspice for about 15 minutes.

Add the rice and a pinch of salt and simmer, covered, for 18 minutes or until the rice is just tender.

Mix the lentils and rice with the chopped fried onion and the remaining oil and season with salt and pepper to taste.

Serve warm or cold with the caramelized onions sprinkled on top.

2 LARGE CARROTS, CUT INTO
3/4-INCH SLICES

1 MEDIUM CELERY ROOT, PEELED
AND CUT INTO 3/4-INCH CUBES

1 MEDIUM SWEET POTATO, PEELED
AND CUT INTO 3/4-INCH CUBES

6 TABLESPOONS LIGHT EXTRA
VIRGIN OLIVE OIL

JUICE OF 1/2 LEMON

SALT AND PEPPER

1 TO 2 TEASPOONS SUGAR

2 TABLESPOONS CHOPPED FRESH
DILL

ROOT VEGETABLES
IN OLIVE OIL

**Vegetables cooked together in a mixture
of olive oil and water with herbs, and served
at room temperature, are a specialty of the eastern
Mediterranean. This winter selection has a
wonderful taste and texture.**

SERVES 4 TO 6

Put the vegetables in a large pan with the olive oil and sauté over low heat, turning them occasionally, for 5 minutes.

Add the lemon juice, salt, pepper, and sugar to taste, and just enough water to cover. Simmer for 25 to 30 minutes or until the vegetables are very tender. Cover and cook for 20 minutes, then uncover and simmer to reduce the sauce.

Add the dill toward the end. Remove from the heat, cool to room temperature, and serve.

SOUPS

Soups are always a pleasant way to start a meal, but accompanied with a good slice of bread a soup can be served as a main course or as a meal in itself. In the Mediterranean soups range from light vegetable creams and iced summer soups to aromatic broths with vegetables and rice, and rich and substantial winter combinations with lentils, beans, and chick peas.

1 TO 2 MELONS, TO YIELD ABOUT
2 POUNDS FLESH

1-INCH PIECE GINGER, GRATED (OR
USE THE JUICE, EXTRACTED WITH A
GARLIC PRESS)

1½ TO 2 TABLESPOONS WHITE
WINE VINEGAR

2 TABLESPOONS EXTRA VIRGIN
OLIVE OIL

SALT AND FRESHLY GROUND WHITE
PEPPER TO TASTE

6 TABLESPOONS GROUND BLANCHED
ALMONDS

CHILLED MELON SOUP

**This delicately flavored, refreshing
summer soup is thickened in the traditional
Mediterranean way, with ground
almonds. Choose sweet, ripe cantalopes,
honeydew, or watermelons.**

SERVES 4

Cut away the peel and rind and remove the seeds of the
melon. Using a blender or food processor, liquidize the
melon flesh with the rest of the ingredients, then chill in
the refrigerator. The soup will thicken to a creamy
consistency when the almonds absorb the juice. Serve
cold.

FOR THE SOUP

1 RED BELL PEPPER, CHOPPED

1 TO 3 CLOVES GARLIC, CRUSHED

3 SLICES WHITE BREAD, CRUSTS
REMOVED, DICED

3 1/4 POUNDS RIPE PLUM TOMATOES,
PEELED

6 TABLESPOONS DRY SHERRY OR
WHITE WINE VINEGAR

5 TABLESPOONS EXTRA VIRGIN
OLIVE OIL

SALT AND PEPPER TO TASTE

1 TO 2 TEASPOONS SUGAR

FOR THE GARNISH

12 ICE CUBES

1 MEDIUM CUCUMBER, PEELED AND
FINELY DICED

1 RED ONION OR 4 SCALLIONS,
CHOPPED

1 GREEN BELL PEPPER, FINELY
DICED

RED GAZPACHO

There are many versions of the famous Andalusian cold soup. This thick, bright red tomato version, with no added water and a generous garnish, is my favorite. It is quite the best thing you could want to eat on a hot summer's day.

SERVES 6 OR MORE

Purée the red bell pepper in a food processor. Add the rest of the soup ingredients and blend to a light, smooth purée, adding a little cold water, if necessary, to thin it. Chill, covered, in the refrigerator.

Serve, adding 2 ice cubes to each soup bowl, accompanied by the garnish ingredients, each on a separate little plate.

3¹/₂ PINTS VEGETABLE STOCK

2 TO 3 MEDIUM LEEKS, CUT INTO
³/₄-INCH SLICES

1 MEDIUM HEAD CELERY WITH
LEAVES, CUT INTO ³/₄-INCH SLICES

1 LARGE POTATO, PEELED AND
DICED

SALT AND FRESHLY GROUND WHITE
PEPPER

3 LARGE CLOVES GARLIC, CHOPPED

JUICE OF 1 TO 3 LEMONS, TO
TASTE

1 TEASPOON SUGAR, OR MORE TO
TASTE

3 MEDIUM ZUCCHINI, CUT INTO
¹/₂-INCH SLICES

6 ARTICHOKE HEARTS (FOR
PREPARATION, SEE PAGE 217), CUT
IN HALF (YOU MAY USE FROZEN
ONES; OPTIONAL)

¹/₂ CUP PINE NUTS OR BLANCHED
ALMONDS, GROUND IN A FOOD
PROCESSOR

2 TABLESPOONS DRIED MINT

1 CUP LONG-GRAIN RICE, COOKED

GREEN VEGETABLE SOUP WITH LEMON

**This is one of my favorite soups that
our family had in Egypt. It is very lemony (its
name, *hamud*, means lemony in Arabic)
and also minty. We made it with chicken stock,
but vegetable stock made with
bouillon cubes will do. Cooked rice is added
at the end, which makes it a
substantial dish. Add the lemon to taste; you
might not like it too acidic. The
pine nuts give a particularly fine flavor.**

SERVES 6 TO 8

In a large pan bring the stock to a boil. Add the leeks, celery, and potato. Add salt and white pepper, garlic, lemon juice, and sugar and simmer for about 30 minutes.

Add the zucchini and artichokes, if using, and simmer for another 15 minutes. Add the ground pine nuts and mint and cook for another 5 to 10 minutes. It is important at this point to taste and adjust the seasoning.

Serve in soup bowls over the hot rice.

1 1/2-POUND PIECE ORANGE
PUMPKIN (WEIGHED WITH THE
SEEDS AND FIBERS REMOVED)

ABOUT 2 LARGE POTATOES, PEELED
AND CUT INTO CUBES

5 CUPS MILK

SALT AND FRESHLY GROUND WHITE
PEPPER

1 TABLESPOON SUGAR, OR TO
TASTE

2 BAY LEAVES

1 SPRIG THYME

2 CINNAMON STICKS

2/3 CUP CRÈME FRAÎCHE, SOUR
CREAM, OR THICK, DRAINED
YOGHURT

PUMPKIN SOUP WITH MILK

**There are pumpkin soups in every
country around the Mediterranean. This lovely
one is from Provence. You can usually get
orange-fleshed pumpkins in Indian and Middle
Eastern stores throughout the year.
Because the taste of pumpkin varies, it is
important to get the right balance of
salt and sugar. Start with a little of each, then
taste, and add more if necessary.**

SERVES 4

Peel the pumpkin and cut the pulp into cubes. Put it in a pan with the potatoes and milk, a pinch of salt, white pepper, sugar, bay leaves, thyme, and cinnamon sticks.

Simmer over low heat, covered, for 20 to 25 minutes, until the potatoes and pumpkin are very soft.

Remove the bay leaves, thyme, and cinnamon sticks and mash the vegetables with a potato masher. Adjust the seasoning and add water to thin the soup if necessary. Cook for 1 to 2 minutes more.

Serve hot, garnished with a dollop of crème fraîche.

ABOUT 2 LARGE POTATOES

2 1/2 PINTS WATER OR VEGETABLE STOCK

1 CUP FRUITY DRY WHITE WINE (OPTIONAL)

9 OUNCES FRESH SHIITAKE MUSHROOMS, CLEANED

2 CLOVES GARLIC, CRUSHED

4 TABLESPOONS LIGHT VEGETABLE OIL

SALT AND PEPPER

1 LARGE BUNCH (ABOUT 3/4 CUP) FLAT-LEAF PARSLEY, FINELY CHOPPED

1 LEMON, CUT INTO WEDGES

2/3 CUP CRÈME FRAÎCHE (OPTIONAL)

MUSHROOM SOUP

This soup, thickened with potato rather than flour, has a wonderfully fresh taste.

SERVES 4

Peel the potatoes and cut them into cubes. Put them in a pan with the water and the wine, if using, and simmer until the potatoes are soft, then mash them with a potato masher.

Chop the mushrooms in a food processor. In a frying pan, sauté the mushrooms and garlic in the oil for 5 minutes, stirring constantly. Pour into the pan with the potatoes.

Add salt and pepper to taste and simmer for 2 to 3 minutes. Just before serving, add the parsley and heat through. Serve accompanied with lemon wedges and, if you like, crème fraîche.

12 OUNCES FRESH SPINACH OR FROZEN LEAF SPINACH

1 MEDIUM ONION, CHOPPED

3 SCALLIONS, FINELY CHOPPED

2 TABLESPOONS SUNFLOWER OR VEGETABLE OIL

1/2 CUP LONG-GRAIN RICE

1/4 TEASPOON TURMERIC (OPTIONAL)

SALT AND FRESHLY GROUND WHITE PEPPER

2 1/4 CUPS YOGHURT

1 CLOVE GARLIC, CRUSHED

SPINACH AND YOGHURT SOUP

You find many different yoghurt soups in the eastern Mediterranean. This hot version is exquisite.

SERVES 4

Wash the spinach and remove the stems only if they are thick and hard. Defrost if using frozen spinach. Drain and cut into strips.

In a large saucepan, sauté the onion and scallions in the oil until soft. Add the rice, and stir to coat it with oil. Pour in 3½ cups water, add the turmeric, if using, season with salt and white pepper to taste and simmer for 15 minutes.

Add the spinach and cook for 5 minutes, or until the rice is tender. The rice should not be too soft and mushy.

Beat the yoghurt together with the garlic, then whisk the mixture into the soup. Heat through but do not boil or the yoghurt will curdle. Serve at once.

1 MEDIUM ONION, CHOPPED

1 SMALL CARROT, FINELY CHOPPED

*1 BUNCH CELERY LEAVES
(1/2 CUP), CHOPPED*

*4 TABLESPOONS SUNFLOWER OR
VEGETABLE OIL*

1 CUP SPLIT RED LENTILS

4 1/2 CUPS VEGETABLE STOCK

SALT AND PEPPER

*3/4 TO 1 TEASPOON GROUND
CUMIN*

JUICE OF 1/2 LEMON

*1 LARGE ONION, SLICED
LENGTHWISE*

VARIATION

Before serving, stir in: 4
chopped garlic cloves fried
in 2 tablespoons olive oil
with 1 teaspoon ground
coriander and 2 teaspoons
dried crumbled mint. A
pinch of dried chili pepper
may be added if you like.

RED LENTIL SOUP

**There are several versions of this
popular Middle Eastern soup. The flavoring
here is rather delicate, but the variation
is more spicy.**

SERVES 4

Sauté the chopped onion, carrot, and celery leaves in
2 tablespoons of the oil in a large saucepan until the
vegetables are soft.

Add the lentils, stock, and salt and pepper to taste
and simmer for 30 to 45 minutes, until the lentils have
disintegrated. Add water if the soup needs thinning, and
stir in the cumin and lemon juice.

Meanwhile, fry the sliced onion in the remaining
oil over medium-high heat, stirring often until crisp and
very brown—almost caramelized.

Serve the soup hot. Garnish each serving with the
fried onions.

1/2 CUP PEARL BARLEY

1 MEDIUM ONION, QUARTERED

1 MEDIUM CARROT, THICKLY SLICED

1 CELERY STALK, THICKLY SLICED

2 CLOVES GARLIC, PEELED

SALT AND PEPPER

14 OUNCES CANNED NAVY OR
CANNELLINI BEANS, DRAINED

2 LEMONS, CUT INTO 6 WEDGES

EXTRA VIRGIN OLIVE OIL

PURÉE OF BEAN AND BARLEY SOUP

This deliciously rich and satisfying soup is from Italy.

SERVES 6

Put the barley in a pan with 4½ cups water. Bring to a boil and skim the surface.

Add the onion, carrot, celery, and garlic and simmer for 1 hour or until the barley is very soft, adding more water if it becomes too dry. Season with salt and pepper to taste.

Pour the soup, in batches, into a food processor or blender with the drained beans and enough water to obtain a creamy soup. Blend until smooth, adding more water if necessary. Return to the pan to heat through.

Serve hot with the lemons and pass around a bottle of olive oil to drizzle into the soup.

1 1/2 CUPS CHICK PEAS, SOAKED IN WATER FOR AT LEAST 1 HOUR OR OVERNIGHT

1 LARGE ONION, COARSELY CHOPPED

1 (14-OUNCE) CAN WHOLE TOMATOES, CHOPPED

3 CELERY STALKS WITH LEAVES, SLICED

2 TABLESPOONS TOMATO PASTE

PEPPER

1/2 TO 3/4 TEASPOON GROUND GINGER

1 TEASPOON CINNAMON

1 CUP LARGE GREEN OR BROWN LENTILS, SOAKED FOR 1 HOUR AND DRAINED

SALT

JUICE OF 1/2 LEMON

ABOUT 4 ZUCCHINI, SLICED

4 OUNCES VERMICELLI, BROKEN INTO BITS BY CRUSHING IN YOUR HANDS

1 LARGE BUNCH (1/2 CUP) FLAT-LEAF PARSLEY, COARSELY CHOPPED

1 LARGE BUNCH (1/2 CUP) CILANTRO, COARSELY CHOPPED

CHICK PEA AND LENTIL SOUP

This rich and filling winter soup is the Moroccan *harira*. It tastes just as good the day after it's made.

SERVES 8 TO 10

Drain the chick peas and put them in a large pan with 5½ pints water, the onion, tomatoes, celery, and tomato paste. Add pepper to taste and simmer, covered, for 1 hour or until the chick peas are very tender.

Add the ginger, cinnamon, and lentils and cook for 20 minutes or until the lentils are soft. Add salt to taste.

Add the lemon juice, zucchini, and vermicelli, and more water if necessary, and cook for 10 minutes. Just before serving, stir in the parsley and cilantro.

SAVORY PIES
AND TARTS

Savory pies and tarts are perfect buffet food and make ideal main dishes for dinner parties. The eastern Mediterranean specializes in pies made with phyllo pastry filled with cheese or spinach, or the more unusual mashed eggplant or pumpkin. The western Mediterranean is famous for its open vegetable tarts, some of the most delightful of which are to be found in the South of France.

1 RECIPE FILLING (CHOOSE ONE
OF THOSE GIVEN ON PAGES 63–5)

4 SHEETS PHYLLO

3 TABLESPOONS MELTED BUTTER OR
VEGETABLE OIL

1 EGG YOLK, MIXED WITH
1 TEASPOON WATER

2 TO 4 TABLESPOONS SESAME
SEEDS (OPTIONAL)

TIP

*There may be problems with the
frozen commercial phyllo. Too
often the sheets are stuck
together and tear when you try
to separate them. A few brands
are invariably good, so when
you find a good one, keep to it.
You can also get the fresh
variety in Greek and Middle
Eastern bakeries and groceries.
If using frozen phyllo, defrost
in its wrapper for 3 hours
before you are ready to use it.*

PHYLLO ROLLS

**A phyllo pie and a salad make an attractive
meal. There are dozens of traditional pies made with
phyllo, with different shapes, sizes, and
fillings, in all the countries that were once part
of the Ottoman Empire.
One of the easiest shapes to prepare is a roll that
can be cut into portions at the table. Fill it with
one of the fillings on the following pages.**

TO MAKE 2 PHYLLO ROLLS TO SERVE 4

Preheat the oven to 350° F.

Prepare one of the fillings and be ready to work
fast with the phyllo. Place one sheet on a flat work
surface. Lightly brush with melted butter or oil. Place
another sheet on top and brush with melted butter or oil.

Spoon half the filling in a fat line along one long
edge, about 1 inch from the edge and 1½ inches from the
two ends. Lift the edge over the filling and very carefully
roll up into a long thin roll, folding the ends in midway
so that the filling does not ooze out. You must do this
quickly because the filling is moist and if it lies too long
on the phyllo, the dough will be too wet to handle.

Brush the top of the roll with the egg yolk and
water mixture and, if you wish, sprinkle with sesame
seeds. Repeat with the remaining filling and dough to
form a second roll.

Bake for 45 minutes, or until crisp and brown.

1 POUND FRESH SPINACH OR
FROZEN WHOLE LEAF SPINACH

3 1/2 OUNCES COTTAGE CHEESE

3 1/2 OUNCES FETA CHEESE,
CRUMBLED

2 EGGS, LIGHTLY BEATEN

SALT, IF NECESSARY, AND PEPPER

A LARGE PINCH NUTMEG

SPINACH FILLING

FILLS 2 ROLLS TO SERVE 4

Wash the fresh spinach, remove the stems only if they are tough, and drain.

Put the leaves in a large pan, and cook, covered, over low heat for a few minutes, until they crumple into a soft mass. Drain and press as much of the water out as you can. If using frozen spinach simply thaw and squeeze all the water out with your hands. If there is liquid, the phyllo will become soggy and tear.

Combine the spinach with the rest of the filling ingredients. When adding salt, take into consideration the saltiness of the feta cheese.

1 POUND MUSHROOMS, SLICED

4 TABLESPOONS VEGETABLE OIL OR
LIGHT EXTRA VIRGIN OLIVE OIL

3 CLOVES GARLIC, CRUSHED

SALT AND PEPPER

4 TABLESPOONS CHOPPED FLAT-
LEAF PARSLEY

4 1/2 OUNCES RICOTTA, DRAINED

MUSHROOM FILLING

**This is an Italian filling used for cannelloni
but it also makes a good filling for a phyllo roll.**

FILLS 2 ROLLS TO SERVE 4

Sauté the mushrooms briefly in the oil with the garlic until tender, adding salt and pepper to taste. Increase the heat to high to reduce the juices. The mushrooms should be almost dry.

Add the parsley and let cool, then mix with the ricotta.

4 1/2 ounces Edam, grated

4 1/2 ounces Gouda, grated

4 1/2 ounces Cheddar, grated

4 1/2 ounces cottage cheese

2 eggs, lightly beaten

Pepper to taste

VARIATIONS

Add 3 tablespoons finely chopped dill or mint and 1/4 teaspoon nutmeg.

Alternative fillings are cottage cheese and feta, or these two with Gruyère.

1 1/2 pounds eggplants

4 1/2 ounces Gruyère, grated

Freshly ground white pepper to taste

1/4 teaspoon nutmeg (optional)

2 eggs, lightly beaten

CHEESE FILLING

Phyllo rolls filled with this mild-tasting concoction can be served as a main course or as a tea-time savory.

FILLS 2 ROLLS TO SERVE 4 TO 8

Put all the ingredients in a food processor and blend to a homogenous paste.

EGGPLANT PURÉE FILLING

FILLS 2 ROLLS TO SERVE 4

Prick the eggplants with a pointed knife in a few places and roast them in a 475° F. oven for 30 minutes, turning them once. Alternatively, put them under the broiler for 15 to 20 minutes, turning them, until the flesh is soft and the skin is blackened.

Peel in a colander and chop the flesh, letting the juices drain out. Mash with a fork, still in the colander, and mix with the rest of the filling ingredients.

2 POUNDS ORANGE PUMPKIN, CUT INTO PIECES

1 CUP FRESHLY GRATED PARMIGIANO-REGGIANO

2 TEASPOONS SUGAR

SALT TO TASTE

2 EGGS, LIGHTLY BEATEN

PUMPKIN FILLING

You can find orange pumpkin in Indian and Middle Eastern stores almost throughout the year. It is sold in slices, with the seeds and fibers removed.

FILLS 2 ROLLS TO SERVE 4

Put the pumpkin in a pan with ½ cup water and cook, covered, for 15 to 20 minutes until the pumpkin is very soft. Drain, return to the pan, and mash with a potato masher or a fork. Cook over a low heat, stirring with a wooden spoon, until the pumpkin has the consistency of a thick paste.

Combine with the rest of the ingredients. When adding salt, take into consideration the saltiness of the cheese.

5 OUNCES FETA CHEESE

5 OUNCES COTTAGE CHEESE

3 EGGS

3 TABLESPOONS CHOPPED FLAT-LEAF PARSLEY

5 SHEETS PHYLLO

2 TABLESPOONS UNSALTED BUTTER, MELTED

1 1/4 CUPS MILK

CREAMY CHEESE BAKE WITH PHYLLO PASTRY

In this version of the Turkish *sutlu borek*, phyllo pastry is baked in a light, creamy custard and becomes soft, like sheets of ever-so-thin pasta. Accompanied with a salad, it makes a scrumptious meal.

SERVES 4

Preheat the oven to 350° F.

To make the filling, mash the feta with a fork and mix with the cottage cheese, 1 egg, and the parsley.

Grease a round baking dish about 12 inches in diameter. Unfold the sheets of phyllo, leaving them in a stack. Brush the top sheet lightly with butter and fit it into the dish buttered side up, bringing the sheet up the sides and folding it. Fit the second sheet over it and brush lightly with butter.

Spread the filling evenly over the dough. Cover with the remaining sheets, brushing each with melted butter and folding them. Fold the top one so that it presents a smooth surface and brush with butter.

Bake for 15 minutes until lightly colored, and remove from the oven.

Lightly beat the remaining 2 eggs with the milk and pour over the hot pie. Return to the oven and bake for about 30 minutes or until the custard is absorbed and set and the top of the pastry is golden.

Serve hot, cut into wedges.

1/2 CUP UNSALTED BUTTER

1 2/3 CUPS ALL-PURPOSE FLOUR

1/4 TEASPOON SALT

1 EGG, LIGHTLY BEATEN

1 TO 2 TABLESPOONS MILK (IF
REQUIRED)

1/2 EGG WHITE (OPTIONAL)

SAVORY SHORTCRUST PASTRY
(TART DOUGH)

**This classic shortcrust pastry works well with all
kinds of fillings, especially those that follow.**

ENOUGH DOUGH FOR 11-INCH TART TO SERVE 6

Cut the butter into small pieces and rub it into the
flour and salt with your hands until it becomes like damp
sand in texture.

Add the egg, mix well, and work very briefly with
your hand until the dough holds together in a soft ball,
adding a little milk if necessary. Cover with plastic wrap
and place in a cool spot for 1 hour.

Preheat the oven to 350° F.

Grease an 11-inch pie pan, a tart pan with a
removable bottom, or flan mold, and line the bottom and
sides with the dough by pressing it in with the palm of
your hands (with this soft dough, it is easier to do this
than to roll it out).

To partially bake the crust before putting in the
filling, prick the bottom in a few places with a fork, brush
with egg white and bake for 10 to 15 minutes. Remove
from the oven and let it cool.

1 LARGE OR 2 SMALL FENNEL BULBS, QUARTERED AND SLICED

SALT

2 EGGS, LIGHTLY BEATEN

1/2 CUP HEAVY CREAM

1/2 CUP MILK

4 OUNCES GRUYÈRE, EMMENTAL, OR FONTINA CHEESE, GRATED

PEPPER

PINCH NUTMEG

1 RECIPE SAVORY SHORTCRUST PASTRY (SEE PAGE 67)

VARIATION

Instead of fennel, use 6 to 8 celery stalks.

CHEESE AND FENNEL TART

The combination of cheese with the delicate flavor of fennel makes a lovely filling.

SERVES 6 TO 8

Preheat the oven to 350° F.

Boil the fennel in lightly salted water until the fennel is soft, then drain.

Beat the eggs with the cream and milk and mix in the cheese, pepper, a pinch of salt (taking into account the saltiness of the cheese), and nutmeg.

Spread the drained fennel pieces in the cooled pastry shell and pour the cheese mixture on top. Bake for 30 minutes and serve hot.

1 POUND SHIITAKE MUSHROOMS

4 TABLESPOONS EXTRA VIRGIN OLIVE OIL

1/2 CUP FRUITY DRY WHITE WINE

SALT AND PEPPER

4 EGGS, LIGHTLY BEATEN

1 SCANT CUP LIGHT CREAM

PINCH NUTMEG

1 RECIPE SAVORY SHORTCRUST PASTRY (SEE PAGE 67)

MUSHROOM TART

**This is a flan in a shortcrust pastry
shell filled with mushrooms with a delicate
wine flavor. I use shiitake mushrooms,
but you may use wild mushrooms, such as
ceps, or a mixture with girolles
and morels if you want to be extravagant.**

SERVES 6

Preheat the oven to 350° F.

Wash and drain the mushrooms. Trim the root ends if necessary. Leave them whole or cut in half if they are very large.

Heat the oil in a large pan over medium heat, add the mushrooms, and sauté for 2 minutes, stirring and turning them over. Add the wine and salt and pepper to taste and cook for about 10 minutes, or until the mushrooms are tender, turning them over gently. Strain the pan juices, which together with the reduced wine should be about 1 scant cup, into a small bowl. Add the eggs and cream to the juices and beat to combine. Add the nutmeg and more salt and pepper to taste.

Arrange the mushrooms in the cooled pastry shell with their tops showing. Pour the egg mixture over and bake for 45 minutes or until the cream has set. Serve hot.

9 OUNCES BOUGHT PUFF PASTRY,
DEFROSTED

1 EGG WHITE

1 LARGE ONION, FINELY CHOPPED

4 TABLESPOONS EXTRA VIRGIN
OLIVE OIL

2 CLOVES GARLIC, FINELY CHOPPED

SALT AND PEPPER

5 RIPE BUT FIRM PLUM TOMATOES,
CUT INTO 1/4-INCH SLICES

1/2 TO 1 TEASPOON SUGAR

12 BASIL LEAVES, SHREDDED

VARIATION

You may use 1 pound
cherry tomatoes cut in half
and arranged with the cut
sides up.

TOMATO TART

**This is a beautiful tart, exquisite and fresh
tasting, and very simple to make.**

SERVES 4

Preheat the oven to 450° F.

Roll out the puff pastry into a round to fit it into a
12-inch tart pan. (This pastry shrinks quite a bit and will
turn out much smaller when it is baked, even if you let it
hang over the sides.) Put it in the refrigerator for 30
minutes.

Brush the pastry with half the egg white (this
prevents it from getting too soggy), prick the bottom all
over with a fork (so that it puffs up evenly), and bake for
10 minutes or until it puffs up and is golden. Take it out,
turn it over, brush the other side with the remaining egg
white and return it to the oven for another 8 minutes or
until the top is crisp and brown. Let it cool.

Fry the onion in 2 teaspoons oil until soft. Add the
garlic and fry, stirring until golden. Remove from the
heat and cool. Spread the onion mixture over the baked
pastry shell. Sprinkle very lightly with salt and pepper.

Arrange the tomato slices on top of the onions so
that they overlap in circles. Brush with the remaining
olive oil and sprinkle lightly with salt, pepper, and sugar.

Place the tart in the oven and bake for 15 to 20
minutes. Sprinkle with the basil and serve hot.

PASTA

A century and a half ago, the foods of Bologna—the pastas with meat sauces in particular—came to represent the ideal Italian cuisine. Pellegrino Artusi, the author of Italy's most famous cookery book, *La scienza in cucina e l'arte di mangiare bene* (Science in the Kitchen and the Art of Eating Well), published in 1891, told his readers to "take a bow when you meet Bolognese cooking." Even in the fifties and sixties Bolognese cooks were still winning all the prizes, but these days it is the vegetable and seafood pastas of southern Italy and Sicily that are fashionable.

1 POUND SHIITAKE MUSHROOMS, OR A MIXTURE OF WILD MUSHROOMS

1 MEDIUM ONION, CHOPPED

3 TABLESPOONS EXTRA VIRGIN OLIVE OIL

1 CLOVE GARLIC, FINELY CHOPPED

JUICE OF 1/2 LEMON

2/3 CUP DRY WHITE WINE

A FEW SPRIGS MARJORAM, CHOPPED

SALT AND PEPPER

1 CUP HEAVY CREAM

14 OUNCES TAGLIATELLE OR TAGLIERINI

PASTA AND MUSHROOMS

Wild mushrooms make this a royal dish but they are costly. Shiitake mushrooms are a good alternative.

SERVES 4

Wash the mushrooms and trim the root ends if necessary. Cut very large ones into 1-inch pieces.

Sauté the onion in the oil over medium heat. Add the mushrooms and garlic and cook until the juices have nearly evaporated, about 5 minutes. Add the lemon juice, wine, marjoram, and salt and pepper to taste and cook for 2 minutes. Add the cream and cook until the sauce is thick.

Cook the pasta in boiling salted water until *al dente*, drain, and serve at once with the sauce spooned on top.

1 MEDIUM ONION, CHOPPED

4 TABLESPOONS OLIVE OIL

1/2 SMALL HEAD ROMAINE LETTUCE, SHREDDED

1/2 CUP VEGETABLE STOCK OR WHITE WINE

1 POUND FRESH SHELLED OR FROZEN PETITS POIS, DEFROSTED

1 POUND FRESH SHELLED OR FROZEN FAVA BEANS, DEFROSTED

2 TEASPOONS DRIED CRUSHED MINT

SALT AND PEPPER

4 FROZEN ARTICHOKE HEARTS OR BOTTOMS, QUARTERED

14 OUNCES PASTA

GRATED PARMIGIANO-REGGIANO

PASTA WITH PEAS, FAVA BEANS, AND ARTICHOKES

SERVES 4

Fry the onion in 2 tablespoons of the oil until soft. Add the lettuce and sauté until it wilts. Add the stock, peas, beans, and mint. Season with salt and pepper to taste and simmer for a few minutes until the vegetables are just tender. Add the artichokes and heat through.

Cook the pasta in boiling salted water until *al dente*, drain, and mix with the remaining oil. Serve with the sauce poured over. Accompany with grated cheese.

1 LARGE EGGPLANT, CUT INTO
3/4-INCH CUBES

SALT

2 BELL PEPPERS, 1 YELLOW AND
1 RED

OLIVE OIL

3 CLOVES GARLIC, PEELED AND
CHOPPED

ABOUT 6 MEDIUM TOMATOES,
PEELED AND COARSELY CHOPPED

PEPPER

1 1/2 TEASPOONS SUGAR

8 BLACK OLIVES, PITTED AND
CHOPPED

1 TABLESPOON CAPERS, DRAINED
OF EXCESS VINEGAR

3 TABLESPOONS SHREDDED OR
TORN BASIL LEAVES

14 OUNCES SPAGHETTI

FRESHLY GRATED PECORINO
ROMANO OR PARMIGIANO-
REGGIANO (OPTIONAL)

SPAGHETTI WITH BELL PEPPERS
AND EGGPLANTS

**This Sicilian pasta is called *Vesuvio*
because the colors resemble the lava
boiling out of the volcano.**

SERVES 4

Sprinkle the eggplant generously with salt and leave in
a colander to drain for 1 hour to degorge their juices,
then rinse and pat dry with a cloth.

Roast the peppers (see page 216). When cool
enough to handle, peel and seed them and cut into strips.

Fry the eggplant cubes in hot oil briefly until
tender and lightly browned, turning them over once,
then drain on paper towels.

In a large pan, fry the garlic in 2 tablespoons oil
until it begins to color. Add the tomatoes, season to taste
with salt, pepper, and sugar and simmer for 15 minutes.

Meanwhile, boil the spaghetti in plenty of salted
water until *al dente*, then drain.

Just before you are ready to serve, add the olives,
capers, eggplant, bell peppers, and basil to the tomato
sauce, and heat through. Pour over the pasta.

Serve with the cheese on the side.

1 POUND FRESH SPINACH OR FROZEN WHOLE LEAF SPINACH

2 CLOVES GARLIC, CRUSHED

2 TABLESPOONS SUNFLOWER OIL

SALT AND PEPPER

3/4 CUP HEAVY CREAM

3 TO 4 TABLESPOONS PINE NUTS, RAW OR TOASTED

14 OUNCES GREEN LINGUINE

SALT

4 TABLESPOONS BUTTER, CUT INTO PIECES

FRESHLY GRATED PARMIGIANO-REGGIANO OR PECORINO ROMANO

GREEN LINGUINE WITH SPINACH AND PINE NUTS

SERVES 4

Wash and drain the spinach. Remove the stems only if they are tough. If using frozen spinach, defrost.

In a very large pan over medium heat, sauté the garlic in the oil until golden, then add the fresh spinach. Put the lid on and let the spinach cook by steaming in the water that clings to it, stirring occasionally. As soon as it crumples into a soft mass—it does so very quickly—remove the pan from the heat. (Frozen spinach needs only a few minutes cooking.)

Season with salt and pepper to taste, and stir in the cream and pine nuts.

Drop the linguine into plenty of vigorously boiling salted water and cook until *al dente*. Drain and serve mixed with the butter and topped with the spinach.

Accompany with grated cheese.

1 1/2 POUNDS CHERRY TOMATOES,
CUT IN HALF

SALT

3 TO 4 CLOVES GARLIC, CHOPPED

1 TO 1 1/2 SMALL HOT RED CHILI
PEPPERS, SEEDED AND CHOPPED
(OPTIONAL)

1/2 CUP EXTRA VIRGIN OLIVE OIL

4 SUN-DRIED TOMATOES, FINELY
SLICED (OPTIONAL)

1 LARGE BUNCH (3/4 TO 1 CUP)
MIXED FRESH HERBS SUCH AS BASIL,
MARJORAM, OREGANO, MINT,
CHERVIL, CHIVES, AND TARRAGON,
CHOPPED

14 OUNCES SPAGHETTI OR
OTHER LONG PASTA

FRESHLY GRATED PECORINO
ROMANO OR PARMIGIANO-
REGGIANO

SPAGHETTI WITH HERBS AND ROASTED CHERRY TOMATOES

SERVES 4

Cook the tomatoes, cut side up, under the broiler, until they soften slightly, and sprinkle very lightly with salt.

For the sauce, fry the garlic and chili peppers in 2 tablespoons of the oil until the aroma rises, then remove from the heat. Add the remaining olive oil, the sun-dried tomatoes, and herbs.

Cook the pasta in boiling salted water until *al dente* and drain. Mix with the sauce and serve topped with the broiled cherry tomatoes. Accompany with grated cheese.

GRAINS:
BULGHUR, RICE, AND COUSCOUS

Wheat, along with the olive tree and the grape vine, was part of the famous triad that the Greeks and Romans planted throughout the ancient world, and is eaten today in the form of pasta, bulghur (cracked wheat) in the eastern Mediterranean, and couscous in North Africa. But while bulghur is the staple food of the eastern Mediterranean countryside, in the cities it is rice, first introduced by the Arabs, that is the everyday fare.

12 OUNCES EGGPLANT, CUT INTO
1 1/4-INCH CUBES

SALT

1 1/2 LARGE ONIONS, SLICED

SUNFLOWER OR LIGHT VEGETABLE
OIL

2 CUPS BULGHUR, PREFERABLY
COARSELY GROUND

3 1/4 CUPS BOILING WATER OR
VEGETABLE STOCK

PEPPER

9 OUNCES HALUMI CHEESE, CUBED

BULGHUR WITH CHEESE
AND EGGPLANT

**This Syrian dish, which combines bulghur
with the chewy, salty *halumi* cheese and eggplant,
can be served as a main course.**

SERVES 4 TO 6

Sprinkle the eggplant generously with salt and leave in
a colander for 1 hour to degorge the juices, then rinse
and pat dry with a cloth.

Fry the onions in 2 tablespoons of oil over medium
heat until golden. Add the bulghur and boiling water.
Season with salt and pepper to taste and stir well, then
cook, covered, over very low heat for about 15 minutes, or
until the water has been absorbed and the bulghur is
tender.

Fry the eggplant briefly in hot oil, turning the
pieces so they are tender and lightly colored on all sides.
Lift out and drain on paper towels.

Stir 5 tablespoons oil into the pan with the bulghur.
Add the halumi cheese and the eggplant and gently mix
them in. Cook over low heat, covered, until the mixture
is heated through and the cheese has melted. Serve at
once.

1 MEDIUM ONION, CHOPPED

5 TABLESPOONS SUNFLOWER OR VEGETABLE OIL

1 1/2 CUPS BULGHUR, PREFERABLY COARSELY GROUND

4 MEDIUM TOMATOES, PEELED AND CHOPPED

2 1/4 CUPS VEGETABLE STOCK

SALT AND PEPPER

2 TABLESPOONS CHOPPED FRESH MINT

BULGHUR PILAF WITH TOMATOES

This can be served as an accompaniment to fish or mixed vegetable dishes.

SERVES 4

Fry the onion in 2 tablespoons of the oil until the onion is soft. Add the bulghur, tomatoes, stock, salt and pepper to taste, and the mint. Stir well and cook, covered, for 15 minutes or until the liquid is absorbed and holes appear on the surface. Add the remaining oil, then turn off the heat and let sit, covered, for 20 minutes. Serve hot.

2¼ CUPS VEGETABLE STOCK

5 TABLESPOONS SUNFLOWER OR
VEGETABLE OIL

1½ CUPS BULGHUR, PREFERABLY
COARSELY GROUND

2 TABLESPOONS RAISINS

SALT AND PEPPER

3 TABLESPOONS PINE NUTS

BULGHUR PILAF WITH
RAISINS AND PINE NUTS

**This is another side dish that can
be served with vegetarian flans and gratins,
egg and cheese dishes, and mixed
vegetables. It also goes well with fish dishes.**

SERVES 4

Bring the stock and 4 tablespoons of the oil to a boil. Add the bulghur, raisins, and salt and pepper to taste (you may not need any salt as the stock is already salty).

Stir well and cook, covered, for 15 minutes or until the liquid is absorbed and holes appear on the surface. Turn off the heat and let sit, covered, for 20 minutes.

Sauté the pine nuts in the remaining oil over medium heat, shaking the pan, until they are lightly golden. Stir them into the bulghur and serve.

1 CLOVE GARLIC, FINELY CHOPPED

2 TABLESPOONS EXTRA VIRGIN OLIVE OIL

ABOUT 6 MEDIUM TOMATOES, PEELED AND CHOPPED

ABOUT 3/4 CUP DRY WHITE WINE

SALT AND PEPPER

1 TO 2 TEASPOONS SUGAR, OR TO TASTE

1 1/4 CUPS ARBORIO RICE

TOMATO RISOTTO

There is a version of rice cooked with tomatoes in almost every country around the Mediterranean. This Provençal method uses wine to give a delicious flavor. It is a good accompaniment to vegetable flans and gratins, egg dishes, cheese bakes, and mixed vegetables, and it also makes a hearty first course.

SERVES 4

In a large pan over medium heat, fry the garlic in the oil until it begins to color. Add the tomatoes, wine, salt, pepper, and sugar to taste and simmer for 15 minutes.

Add the rice and cook, covered, over very low heat, for about 20 minutes, until the rice is creamy but still *al dente*. Add a little more wine if it becomes too dry.

Serve hot or at room temperature.

1 POUND FRESH SPINACH

1 LARGE ONION, CHOPPED

4 TABLESPOONS LIGHT VEGETABLE OIL

1 1/2 CUPS LONG-GRAIN RICE

2 1/4 CUPS VEGETABLE STOCK OR WATER

SALT AND PEPPER

1 TEASPOON SUGAR

JUICE OF 1/2 LEMON, OR TO TASTE

YOGHURT (OPTIONAL)

RICE WITH SPINACH

This beautiful Turkish pilaf is often accompanied with yoghurt. It can be served, like the other rice side dishes, with most vegetable dishes and can also be a first course.

SERVES 4

Wash and drain the spinach, and chop coarsely or leave whole. Remove the stems only if they are tough.

Fry the onion in the oil in a large pan over medium heat until soft.

Add the rice and stir well to coat. Add the stock, salt, pepper, sugar, and lemon juice to taste, and the spinach. Stir well and cook, covered, over very low heat for about 18 minutes, or until the rice is tender.

Serve hot or cold. Accompany with yoghurt, if you like. For extra flavor, add crushed garlic to the yoghurt.

NOTE Frozen leaf spinach, defrosted and coarsely chopped, may be used.

1 LARGE ONION, CHOPPED

1/2 CUP SUNFLOWER OIL

4 TABLESPOONS PINE NUTS

1 1/4 CUPS LONG-GRAIN RICE

SALT

1/2 TEASPOON CINNAMON

1/4 TEASPOON ALLSPICE

1/4 TEASPOON GROUND CARDAMOM

2 CUPS BOILING VEGETABLE STOCK OR WATER

2 TO 3 TABLESPOONS CURRANTS OR RAISINS

VARIATION

Mix in at the end a small can of chick peas, drained, boiled briefly in water, and then drained again.

RICE PILAF WITH RAISINS AND PINE NUTS

This is the standard pilaf found in Middle Eastern restaurants and cafeterias. It makes a good side dish for many of the vegetable dishes and can also be served cold.

SERVES 4

Fry the onion in about half the oil over medium heat until they are soft. Add the pine nuts and cook, stirring, until they are lightly browned all over.

Add the rice and stir to coat the grains with oil. Add salt to taste, cinnamon, allspice, and cardamom.

Pour in the boiling stock to cover, add the currants, and mix well. Cook, covered, for 18 to 20 minutes, until the rice is tender.

Stir in the remaining oil and serve hot or at room temperature.

1 LARGE ONION, CHOPPED

4 TABLESPOONS BUTTER

1 TABLESPOON VEGETABLE OIL

1 1/2 CUPS ARBORIO RICE

2 1/4 CUPS DRY WHITE WINE

SALT AND PEPPER

2 1/4 CUPS VEGETABLE STOCK MADE WITH 1 BOUILLON CUBE

2 CUPS SHELLED BABY PEAS

9 OUNCES ASPARAGUS TIPS

2/3 CUP HEAVY CREAM (OPTIONAL)

4 TABLESPOONS FRESHLY GRATED PARMIGIANO-REGGIANO (OPTIONAL)

VARIATION

Other vegetables could be added, such as boiled sliced fennel or celery, sliced zucchini, or fava beans.

RISOTTO WITH PEAS AND ASPARAGUS

This Italian springtime risotto is light and fresh. I prefer it without the cream and cheese but some of my family prefer the richer version. Serve it as a first course or as a main dish.

SERVES 4 TO 6

In a large frying pan or sauté pan, fry the onion in half the butter and all of the oil, over very low heat, until soft, stirring occasionally.

Add the rice and stir until all the grains are coated and become translucent. Pour in the wine, season with salt and pepper to taste, and simmer gently until the wine is absorbed.

Gradually stir in the stock, a little at a time, adding more as it becomes absorbed, and water if necessary, until the rice is creamy but still *al dente*.

Meanwhile, cook the peas and asparagus in boiling salted water until they are just tender, and drain.

Stir the remaining butter, the cream, and cheese, if using, into the rice, and serve at once, topped with the vegetables.

Couscous

**Couscous is the indigenous Berber food of
North Africa. The word refers to the hard semolina
grain on which it is based as well as to the
stew or soup and the side dishes that go with it. In
North Africa, couscous is served at the end of a
festive meal, before the sweet, or as a one-dish family
meal. Stews and soups are nearly always based
on meat or chicken, and sometimes fish (see Fish
Couscous with Quince on page 167).
A stew with only vegetables is considered a dish *de
regime* for people on a diet. But with a good
assortment of vegetables, it can be a truly glorious
affair—a joy to look at and a pleasure to eat.
The combination of many different herbs and sweet
spices is part of the appeal.**

BASIC METHOD FOR MAKING COUSCOUS

The couscous we buy in most grocery stores is
precooked. All you do is add salted water and oil and heat
it through. When I visited a couscous factory in Sfax,
Tunisia, the owner explained that their couscous could
be heated in a saucepan on the stove top, in the oven, or
in the microwave.

I shamelessly make it the easiest way, as prescribed
in the packet instructions, with very good results. It is so
easy you can make it for very large parties. Simply
measure the volume of the grain and add the same

LEFT Vegetable Couscous (page 96)

volume of warm water—even a little less, as you can add more later if necessary.

For 6 to 8 people put 2½ cups medium-ground couscous in a bowl. Add 2½ cups warm water with ½ to 1 teaspoon salt, stirring slowly so that the water is absorbed evenly.

After about 10 to 15 minutes, when the couscous has become a little plump and tender, add 3 to 4 tablespoons peanut or light vegetable oil and rub the grain between your hands to air it and break up any lumps. Heat it through by steaming in the top part of a couscoussier (it is ready as soon as the steam passes through the grain) or, more simply, in the oven, covered with foil, at 400° F. for about 20 minutes.

When I make couscous for a large number of people, I put it straight into the huge clay dish I plan to serve it in, which goes into the oven. There is nothing easier.

A small quantity for 2 or 3 people can be heated in a saucepan, stirring to prevent it from burning. Before serving, break up any lumps very thoroughly.

1 RECIPE BROILED OR ROASTED
VEGETABLES (SEE PAGE 102)

2¹/₂ CUPS COUSCOUS

3³/₄ CUPS WATER

1¹/₂ VEGETABLE BOUILLON CUBES

A PINCH SALT

1 TO 2 CLOVES GARLIC, CRUSHED

¹/₂ TO 1 TEASPOON CINNAMON

¹/₄ TEASPOON ALLSPICE

¹/₄ TEASPOON POWDERED GINGER

¹/₄ TEASPOON GROUND SAFFRON
(OPTIONAL)

A LARGE PINCH CHILI POWDER

4 TABLESPOONS CHOPPED CILANTRO

2 TABLESPOONS CHOPPED FLAT-LEAF
PARSLEY

4 TABLESPOONS SUNFLOWER OR
VEGETABLE OIL

2 TABLESPOONS RAISINS, SOAKED IN
WATER FOR 10 MINUTES

COUSCOUS WITH
ROASTED VEGETABLES

**This is not a traditional North African
dish but it is most appealing. Because the roast
vegetables have no broth, I have devised a
way of treating the grain so that it is moist and
aromatic without the traditional soup.**

SERVES 6

Put the couscous in a large, ovenproof serving dish.

In a large pot, bring the water to a boil. Add the bouillon cubes, salt (take into consideration the saltiness of the bouillon cubes), garlic, cinnamon, allspice, ginger, saffron, and chili powder. Simmer for 8 minutes, until the garlic is soft. Remove from the heat and add the cilantro and parsley.

Pour 2¹/₂ cups of this hot soup over the couscous (keep the rest to moisten the grain when you are serving) and stir well so that it is absorbed evenly. Let soak for 15 minutes or until the grain is tender. Stir in the oil and rub the grain between your palms to fluff it up and separate and break up any lumps. Drain the raisins and add them to the couscous.

About 20 minutes before serving, heat the grain through, covered with foil, in a 400° F. oven.

Reheat the soup and the vegetables. Break up any lumps in the couscous and serve with the remaining soup poured over and the vegetables on top.

FOR THE GARNISH

1 1/4 CUPS CHICK PEAS, SOAKED FOR
AT LEAST 1 HOUR

SALT

1 CUP RAISINS

FOR THE COUSCOUS

5 CUPS COUSCOUS

5 CUPS WATER

1 TO 2 TEASPOONS SALT

6 TABLESPOONS PEANUT
OR VEGETABLE OIL

AROMATICS

SALT AND PEPPER TO TASTE

2 TEASPOONS CINNAMON

1/2 TEASPOON ALLSPICE

3/4 TEASPOON GROUND GINGER

1/2 TEASPOON SAFFRON POWDER

1/4 TEASPOON CHILI POWDER

1 BUNCH (3/4 CUP) FLAT-LEAF
PARSLEY, CHOPPED

1 BUNCH (3/4 CUP) CILANTRO,
CHOPPED

1 BUNCH (1/2 CUP) ARUGULA,
COARSELY CHOPPED

1 BUNCH (1/2 CUP) WATERCRESS,
COARSELY CHOPPED

2 TEASPOONS HARISSA (SEE PAGE
219) OR MORE TO TASTE, OR 2
TEASPOONS PAPRIKA AND 1/4 TO
1/2 TEASPOON OR MORE CHILI
POWDER

VEGETABLE COUSCOUS

The following recipe is for 10 or more
because it is as easy to make for many as it is for
a few and it is a good party dish. It can also be
made in advance. It might seem daunting because
of the number of ingredients but it is simply
a matter of throwing vegetables into a pot.
I give a long list of vegetables to choose from. Seven
is the usual lucky number, but you can have as
many as you like and you can vary the quantities.

SERVES 10 TO 12

To make the garnish, boil the chick peas in water for 1
hour or until tender, adding a pinch of salt when they
begin to soften. Boil the raisins separately for 15 minutes
in enough water to cover.

Preheat the oven to 400° F.

Prepare the couscous grain, as described on page
93, in an ovenproof serving dish. About 20 to 30 minutes
before serving, cover the dish with foil and heat through
in the oven (it will steam).

To prepare the stew or soup, put 4 1/2 pints water
with 7 (or more) vegetables of your choice in a large
saucepan. Bring to a boil and skim the surface. Add salt
and pepper and the spices (but not the herbs or Harissa)
and simmer for 30 minutes or until all the vegetables are
tender. Add the herbs and cook for 5 minutes.

To make the peppery sauce, put 2 ladlesful of liquid
from the soup in a small bowl and stir in the Harissa or
paprika and chili powder.

Before serving, break up any lumps in the couscous very thoroughly, stir in a little of the broth, and shape the grain into a mound. Serve the vegetables in a separate bowl or arrange them on top of the couscous. Reheat the chick peas and raisins and put them into separate bowls. Serve them on the side along with the peppery sauce.

MIXED VEGETABLE DISHES

The wide range of Mediterranean vegetables and the magnificent flavor they acquire under the warm sun are legendary. The art of cooking them the Mediterranean way—a rich amalgam of food traditions inherited from the ancient world, from the Byzantine and Ottoman Empires, the Middle East, France, Italy, and Spain—has been carried to all the corners of the world. Many of the dishes in this section are ideal party food. They can be served as side dishes and they also make spectacular main dishes, served simply with bread and cheese.

FOR THE COOKING
LIQUOR

1 (750-ML) BOTTLE DRY WHITE
WINE

3/4 CUP VERY LIGHT, MILD-TASTING
EXTRA VIRGIN OLIVE OIL

SALT TO TASTE

2 SPRIGS THYME

4 BAY LEAVES

SUGGESTIONS

*You can use asparagus,
scallions, shiitake mushrooms,
green beans, snow peas, tiny
onions, carrots, potatoes,
parsnips, and turnips. To my
surprise, my favorites for this
treatment were carrots,
potatoes, and parsnips. Most
vegetables are best left whole.
Large carrots can be cut into
thick slices or in half
lengthwise, and turnips,
parsnips, and potatoes, cut into
slices or cubed.*

VEGETABLES COOKED IN WHITE WINE AND OLIVE OIL

**This Provençal method of cooking vegetables,
in a mixture of white wine (I use a fruity dry
Riesling) and olive oil, gives them a splendid flavor,
and to some, a soft, muted gold color.
They retain a certain firmness of texture even
when they are long-cooked.
A beautiful assortment makes a grand party dish
to serve hot or at room temperature.
You must cook the vegetables separately, giving each
the time they require, which is longer than
is needed in boiling water. Asparagus and scallions,
for instance, take about 10 minutes;
carrots and potatoes 45 to 60 minutes. Let them
simmer gently over low heat with the lid on.**

Put the wine and oil in a large pan with salt, thyme, and bay leaves. Bring to a boil (oil will combine with the wine as the mixture bubbles) then simmer over low heat. Cook the vegetables in batches, lifting them out and arranging them on a serving platter as they become tender. If you want to serve them hot, heat through in the oven, covered with foil. I particularly like them at room temperature.

4 POUNDS BABY VEGETABLES OR
NEW SPRING VEGETABLES SUCH AS
TINY NEW POTATOES, SCALLIONS,
ASPARAGUS SPEARS, BABY
ZUCCHINI, TINY LEEKS, SMALL
FENNEL BULBS OR CELERY HEARTS,
PEARL ONIONS, GREEN BEANS,
SNOW PEAS, BABY LETTUCES, AND
SWEET CORN

ABOUT 3¹/₂ PINTS VEGETABLE STOCK

SALT TO TASTE

2 TO 3 CLOVES GARLIC, CHOPPED

4 BAY LEAVES

2 SPRIGS THYME

FOR THE DRESSING

¹/₂ CUP VERY LIGHT, MILD-TASTING
EXTRA VIRGIN OLIVE OIL OR A
MIXTURE OF OLIVE AND SUNFLOWER
OILS

¹/₂ CUP MIXED CHOPPED HERBS
SUCH AS CHERVIL, CHIVES, AND
PARSLEY

BABY VEGETABLES
COOKED IN STOCK

**About 10 years ago the chefs of Provence brought into
fashion tiny baby vegetables and have since refined
their ways of cooking them. If the variety of
vegetables is large enough, you can serve the dish as
the main part of a meal for four, or pile them onto a
platter as the centerpiece for a dinner party.
Perfectionists boil the vegetables separately
as they cook at slightly different rates, even though
they are all tiny.**

SERVES 4

Leave the vegetables whole and wash them, peel them
(or not, as desired), but leave the little stalks and leaves
if they have them. Trim the roots and dark green ends of
leeks and scallions. Boil the vegetables in enough stock
to cover, with salt if necessary, the garlic, bay leaves, and
thyme, until *al dente*. Drain.

Whisk together the oil and herbs for the dressing
and pour over the vegetables.

VARIATION

To intensify the flavor add
the juice of ¹/₂ lemon and
1 tablespoon sugar to the
stock.

1 LARGE EGGPLANT, CUT INTO
1/2-INCH SLICES LENGTHWISE

SALT

4 MEDIUM ZUCCHINI, CUT INTO
1/2-INCH SLICES LENGTHWISE

2 MEDIUM MILD ONIONS, CUT INTO
THICK SLICES

2 TO 4 PLUM TOMATOES, CUT IN
HALF

2 RED OR YELLOW BELL PEPPERS,
CUT IN HALF

EXTRA VIRGIN OLIVE OIL

4 TO 8 LARGE CLOVES GARLIC IN
THEIR SKINS

PEPPER

4 TABLESPOONS CHOPPED HERBS
SUCH AS PARSLEY, MARJORAM,
BASIL, OR CHERVIL (OPTIONAL)

VARIATIONS

If you serve the vegetables cold, you may wish to squeeze a little lemon juice over them or sprinkle with a little sweet sherry or balsamic vinegar.

Boil 14 ounces pasta in salted water until *al dente*, then drain. Dress with 6 tablespoons or more extra virgin olive oil mixed with 6 tablespoons chopped flat-leaf parsley and serve topped with the roasted vegetables.

BROILED OR ROASTED VEGETABLES

Vegetables cooked on a barbecue, under the broiler, or roasted at high heat in the oven, develop a rich, intense flavor. All kinds of vegetables may be broiled, but those listed (left) are a typical Mediterranean combination. This recipe makes a wonderful meal in itself. The same roasted vegetables can be served over a couscous base (see page 93) or with pasta.

SERVES 4

Sprinkle the eggplant slices generously with salt and leave in a colander to drain for 30 minutes to degorge their juices, then rinse and pat dry with a cloth.

Brush the eggplant, zucchini, onions, tomatoes, and peppers with oil.

Cook the eggplant, zucchini, and onions on the barbecue or under the broiler, until the insides are tender and the outsides are browned, turning them over once. Cook the peppers with the skin side only towards the fire. Cook the tomatoes and garlic until softened.

Alternatively, roast the sliced vegetables on baking sheets lined with foil in a very hot (475° F.) oven, being careful that they do not overcook.

Arrange all the vegetables on a serving plate. The garlic cloves can be peeled or left in their skins.

Serve hot or cold, sprinkled with salt and pepper, a drizzle of olive oil, and, if you like, chopped parsley or other fresh herbs such as marjoram, basil, or chervil.

2 MEDIUM ONIONS

2 RED BELL PEPPERS

2 MEDIUM EGGPLANTS

2 PLUM TOMATOES

1 WHOLE HEAD GARLIC WITH LARGE CLOVES

4 TO 5 TABLESPOONS OLIVE OIL

SALT AND PEPPER

WHOLE ROASTED VEGETABLES

This is another popular way of cooking vegetables in the Mediterranean—a plateful of these vegetables, served with an assortment of good cheeses, makes a perfect meal.

SERVES 4

Preheat the oven to 350° F. Prick the eggplants with a sharp knife to prevent them from bursting. Put all the vegetables whole, as they are, on baking sheets lined with foil. Roast them in the oven until soft. Take the tomatoes and garlic out after 20 minutes, when they soften. Cook the onions, peppers, and eggplants for about 1 hour, until the skins are brown, turning them once.

Drop the peppers into a heavy-duty plastic bag and twist to seal it (this loosens the skin). When they are cool enough to handle, peel the vegetables and seed the peppers. Cut the tomatoes in half, the onions in quarters, the bell peppers and eggplants into strips. Peel the garlic cloves and leave them whole.

Dress with the olive oil and salt and pepper to taste and toss the vegetables together. Serve warm or at room temperature.

4 SMALL TURNIPS

1 LARGE PARSNIP

1 LARGE CARROT

1 SWEET POTATO

2 TABLESPOONS SUNFLOWER OR
VEGETABLE OIL

STOCK MADE WITH 2¼ CUPS
WATER AND 1 VEGETABLE BOUILLON
CUBE

1½ CUPS DRY WHITE WINE
(OPTIONAL)

SALT AND PEPPER TO TASTE

1 TABLESPOON LEMON JUICE

16 CHESTNUTS

ROOT VEGETABLES
WITH CHESTNUTS

**It is worth making use of chestnuts
in this engaging French preparation. You can use
either frozen or vacuum-packed ones.**

SERVES 4

Peel the vegetables, cut them into 1-inch cubes, and put them in a pot.

Add the oil, stock, and wine, if using, to cover. Season with salt and plenty of pepper, taking into consideration the saltiness of the stock, and add the lemon juice.

Simmer over low heat, uncovered, for about 25 minutes, or until the vegetables are just tender and the liquid is reduced to a sauce.

Meanwhile, prepare the chestnuts. To peel them, make a slit in their flat side with a pointed knife and roast them under the broiler for 2 minutes, turning them over once, until they blacken slightly. Peel them as soon as they are cool enough to handle. Drop them into the pan with the vegetables and cook in the sauce for 5 minutes or longer. Raise the heat to high, if necessary, to reduce the sauce.

Serve hot.

FOR THE BATTER

1 CUP ALL-PURPOSE FLOUR

1/2 TEASPOON SALT

1 TEASPOON BAKING POWDER

1 TABLESPOON EXTRA VIRGIN OLIVE OIL

1 EGG YOLK

ABOUT 3/4 CUP WATER OR SODA WATER

FOR THE VEGETABLES

CHOOSE A VARIETY FROM THE FOLLOWING: LARGE SCALLIONS, TRIMMED OF THEIR ROOTS AND DARK GREEN ENDS; ASPARAGUS, TRIMMED OF THEIR TOUGH ENDS; BUTTON MUSHROOMS; ZUCCHINI, SLICED LENGTHWISE; EGGPLANTS, SLICED INTO 1/2-INCH-THICK ROUNDS; CAULIFLOWER, BLANCHED AND CUT INTO FLORETS; ARTICHOKE BOTTOMS, SLICED

SUNFLOWER OIL FOR DEEP FRYING

SALT AND PEPPER TO TASTE

1 LEMON, CUT INTO WEDGES

VEGETABLE FRITTERS

Italians are famous for their deep-fried vegetables in batter—*fritti misti di verdura*—which vary in content from one region to another and to which, in the South, they sometimes add breaded pieces of mozzarella, and in the North, lumps of fried, slightly sweet, thick "cream" (actually milk cooked with ground rice), and fruit such as sliced apples. But every other country in the Mediterranean has some version of vegetable fritters too. Turks specialize in fried eggplant and zucchini slices, which they serve with yoghurt or with Fresh Tomato Sauce (see page 218).

Mix the flour, salt, and baking powder in a large bowl and add the oil and egg yolk. Vigorously beat in enough water to make a light, smooth batter. Let rest for 30 minutes and beat again before using.

To make the fritters, cut the vegetables into slices, dip them in the batter and deep-fry in sizzling, medium-hot sunflower oil until crisp and lightly browned, and tender inside. Drain on paper towels and keep warm in the oven.

Serve at once, sprinkled with salt and pepper, and accompanied with lemon wedges. Reheat, if necessary, in the oven.

OVERLEAF From left to right: Mixed Vegetable Fritters; Spaghetti with Bell Peppers and Eggplants (page 75)

ABOUT 5 SMALL TURNIPS, PEELED

1 3/4 CUPS SHELLED FAVA BEANS

1 CLOVE GARLIC, FINELY CHOPPED

3 TABLESPOONS SUNFLOWER OR
VEGETABLE OIL

JUICE OF 1/2 LEMON

1 TO 2 TEASPOONS SUGAR

1 TEASPOON DRIED MINT

9 OUNCES SPINACH

FAVA BEANS, TURNIPS, AND SPINACH

It is best to use fresh vegetables but frozen fava beans and frozen whole leaf spinach will do very well.

SERVES 4 TO 6

Cut the turnips in half then into 1/3-inch slices. Put them in a large pan with the beans, garlic, and oil, and sauté over very low heat for 5 to 10 minutes until lightly colored.

Add the lemon juice, sugar, mint, and about 4 tablespoons water and cook for about 10 to 20 minutes, until the vegetables are tender.

Meanwhile, wash and drain the spinach (remove the stems only if they are tough), and press out the excess water. Put it in the pan on top of the beans and turnips. Put the lid on so that the leaves cook in the steam, until they crumple. Stir well and adjust the seasoning.

Serve hot or cold.

NOTE If using frozen beans and spinach, simply defrost and add to the pan when the turnips are tender, then cook for a few more minutes.

Omelets and Egg Dishes

The Mediterranean is famous for its egg dishes and omelets. The latter are usually like thick cakes, filled with vegetables, and can be eaten hot or cold. Accompanied with salad they make a good family meal, and because they can be made in advance, they are an easy option for entertaining and buffet meals. They are colorful and can look quite elegant, cut into wedges or little squares and garnished with watercress. They are also traditional picnic foods.

9 OUNCES FRESH SPINACH OR
FROZEN WHOLE LEAF SPINACH

1 LARGE ONION, CHOPPED

4 TABLESPOONS SUNFLOWER OR
LIGHT VEGETABLE OIL

1 LARGE TOMATO, PEELED AND
CHOPPED

SALT AND PEPPER

4 EGGS

1/4 TEASPOON NUTMEG

VARIATIONS

A handful of cooked chick
peas or beans may be
added to the omelet
mixture.

For a Provençal omelet,
cook 14 ounces spinach
and mix with 4 large eggs,
a pinch of nutmeg,
1 crushed garlic clove and
4 tablespoons grated
Parmigiano or Gruyère
cheese.

Another French version
adds a handful of cooked
green peas and 2 artichoke
hearts cut into slices.

SPINACH OMELET

**Every Arab country has a version
of spinach omelet. This one is Egyptian.**

SERVES 4

Wash and drain the fresh spinach and squeeze out the
excess water. Remove the stems only if they are tough.
Put it in a saucepan over low heat and cover with the lid.
The spinach will cook in the steam of the water that
clings to it and crumple very quickly to a soft mass. Drain
in a colander and press all the water out.

If using frozen spinach, thaw thoroughly and press
all the water out.

Fry the onion in 2 tablespoons of the oil until
golden. Add the tomato and salt and pepper to taste and
cook for 15 minutes or until the sauce is reduced.

Beat the eggs lightly in a bowl with salt, pepper,
and nutmeg. Add the tomato sauce and the spinach and
mix well.

Heat the rest of the oil in a well-seasoned skillet or
nonstick sauté pan. Pour in the spinach and egg mixture
and cook over a low heat for about 10 minutes until the
bottom has set. Put the skillet under the broiler and cook
until the top is firm and lightly browned.

Serve hot or at room temperature, cut into wedges.

ABOUT 2 MEDIUM EGGPLANTS

1 LARGE ONION, CHOPPED

4 TABLESPOONS OLIVE OIL

3 CLOVES GARLIC, CRUSHED

4 EGGS

1/2 CUP COARSELY CHOPPED FLAT-LEAF PARSLEY

1/2 TO 1 TEASPOON GROUND CARAWAY SEEDS

1/2 TEASPOON GROUND CORIANDER SEEDS

SALT AND PEPPER

1 LEMON, CUT INTO WEDGES

EGGPLANT OMELET

Maacoudes—omelets that combine all kinds of ingredients—are among the most popular hors d'oeuvres in Tunisia. They are served hot or at room temperature. This one has a lovely, subtle texture and flavor. The eggplant is not fried but broiled, so does not absorb any oil.

SERVES 4

Prick the eggplants in a few places with a pointed knife to prevent them from bursting. Put them on a baking sheet under the broiler for about 20 minutes, turning them until their skin is black and the flesh is soft.

Meanwhile, fry the onion in 2 tablespoons of the oil over very low heat until golden, stirring occasionally. Add the garlic and stir until lightly colored.

Put the eggplants in a colander and peel them. Chop the flesh with two knives in the colander, then mash it with a fork, allowing the juices to run out.

In a bowl, beat the eggs lightly. Add the mashed eggplant, the onion, garlic, parsley, caraway, coriander, and salt and pepper to taste. Mix well.

Heat the remaining oil in a large, well-seasoned skillet or nonstick sauté pan. Pour in the mixture and cook, covered, over very low heat for about 10 minutes until the bottom has set. Put the skillet under the broiler and cook until the top is firm and lightly browned.

Serve hot or at room temperature accompanied with lemon wedges.

1 ONION, COARSELY CHOPPED

ABOUT 6 TABLESPOONS EXTRA
VIRGIN OLIVE OIL

2 CLOVES GARLIC, CHOPPED

1 MEDIUM EGGPLANT, CUT INTO
2/3-INCH CUBES

2 MEDIUM ZUCCHINI, CUT INTO
1/2-INCH SLICES

1 RED BELL PEPPER, CUT INTO
2/3-INCH STRIPS

4 MEDIUM TOMATOES, PEELED AND
CHOPPED

SALT AND PEPPER TO TASTE

1 TEASPOON SUGAR

1 SPRIG THYME, CRUMBLED

4 TABLESPOONS CHOPPED PARSLEY

4 EGGS, LIGHTLY BEATEN

FIVE VEGETABLE OMELET

**In the south of France this dish is called a
tian de bohemienne. In North Africa a mixture of
fried vegetables with eggs in a skillet
is called a *shakshouka*. All kinds of vegetables can go
into a *shakshouka*, including peas, fava beans, and
pumpkin, but the most popular combination is that
usually found in a ratatouille mixture. The
French deep-fry the vegetables separately, then drain
them, mix them with the rest of the ingredients,
and bake them, but sautéing them all in the skillet
is quicker and equally good.**

SERVES 4

In a large skillet, fry the onion in 2 tablespoons of the oil until they are soft.

Add the garlic, eggplant, zucchini, bell pepper, and the rest of the oil and sauté over high heat, then medium heat, turning the vegetables over frequently, until lightly colored.

Add the tomatoes, salt and pepper, sugar, and thyme, and cook for a few more minutes.

Add the parsley and eggs, a little more salt and pepper, and cook until the eggs have set.

Serve hot with bread.

2 LARGE POTATOES, PEELED AND CUT INTO ¹/₄-INCH SLICES

1 LARGE SPANISH ONION, THINLY SLICED

SALT

¹/₂ CUP OIL—A MIXTURE OF OLIVE OIL AND LIGHT VEGETABLE OIL

3 EGGS, LIGHTLY BEATEN

SPANISH POTATO TORTILLA

The tortilla is the most popular appetizer served in Spanish tapas bars, but it can also be the center of a family meal. It can be made in advance and reheated or eaten cold.

SERVES 4 TO 5

Sprinkle the potatoes and onion lightly with salt.

Heat the oil in a nonstick skillet and add the potatoes and onion at the same time. Cook slowly over medium heat (it is actually stewing, rather than frying), for about 15 minutes, stirring occasionally, until the vegetables are tender but not brown.

Drain the vegetables in a colander, reserving the oil.

In a bowl, mix the potatoes and onion with the eggs and let soak for about 15 minutes.

Wipe the skillet clean with a paper towel and heat 2 tablespoons of the reserved oil until it is very hot. Pour in the potato and egg mixture and lower the heat to medium-low. Shake the pan occasionally to prevent the tortilla from sticking. When it starts to come away from the sides of the pan and the bottom has browned a little, turn over the tortilla by placing a large plate over the skillet and quickly turning the tortilla upside-down onto it. Add another tablespoon of oil to the skillet and quickly slide the tortilla back in. Cook the other side for a minute. Alternatively, brown under the broiler.

Serve hot or cold, cut into wedges.

3 OR MORE CLOVES GARLIC,
CHOPPED

3 TABLESPOONS SUNFLOWER OR
EXTRA VIRGIN OLIVE OIL

4 PLUM TOMATOES, CUT INTO
1/3-INCH SLICES

SALT AND PEPPER TO TASTE

2/3 TEASPOON SUGAR

4 EGGS

3 TABLESPOONS CHOPPED BASIL,
CILANTRO, OR PARSLEY

VARIATIONS

Peel and chop the tomatoes.
Cook as described in the
recipe; when the tomatoes
have softened, add the eggs
and scramble them gently.
Serve them soft and
creamy.

Add a few pitted, roughly
chopped black olives.

EGG AND TOMATO

**When one of my children arrives unexpectedly
at mealtime, Egg and Tomato, accompanied with
bread, is one of the things I rustle up. It is a
common standby in Egypt. Often, I do not bother to
peel the tomatoes, and it makes no difference
in the end result.**

SERVES 2

In a large skillet, fry the garlic in the oil until it begins
to color.

Add the tomatoes, preferably in one layer, and
season lightly with salt, pepper, and sugar. Cook for 2 to
3 minutes then turn over the tomato slices.

Break open the eggs on top of the tomato mixture
and sprinkle with salt and pepper. Cook over gentle heat
until the eggs have set.

Serve hot, sprinkled with herbs.

2 RED BELL PEPPERS

1 MEDIUM ONION, CHOPPED

2 TABLESPOONS OLIVE OR
SUNFLOWER OIL

ABOUT 6 MEDIUM TOMATOES,
PEELED AND DICED

SALT AND PEPPER

1 TO 2 TEASPOONS SUGAR

2 TABLESPOONS CAPERS (OPTIONAL)

1/2 TO 1 TEASPOON HARISSA,
DILUTED WITH 1 TABLESPOON
WATER (SEE PAGE 219) OR
1 TEASPOON PAPRIKA AND A LARGE
PINCH OF CAYENNE OR RED CHILI
POWDER (OPTIONAL)

4 EGGS, LIGHTLY BEATEN

VARIATIONS

To make it a substantial
dish, add 2 boiled, peeled,
and diced potatoes or a
drained 14-ounce can of
navy beans.

You may also add a handful
of grated Gruyère or
crumbled feta.

EGGS BAKED WITH
PEPPERS AND TOMATOES

**This delectable Tunisian dish is called a *tagine*
after the shallow clay dish in which it is cooked.**

SERVES 4

Preheat the oven to 350° F.

Roast the peppers (for directions see page 216),
peel, and cut into ribbons.

Fry the onion in the oil over medium heat until
golden. Add the tomatoes, salt, pepper, and sugar to
taste and simmer for about 20 minutes until the sauce is
reduced.

Remove from the heat and add the capers and
Harissa. Allow the mixture to cool a little, then beat
in the eggs.

Put the peppers in an oiled baking dish (about 9
inches diameter) and pour the egg mixture on top. Bake
for 50 minutes or until the eggs have set. Serve hot.

FLANS, GRATINS, AND CHEESE BAKES

These baked vegetable dishes with eggs and cheese make ideal vegetarian meals because they contain all the necessary proteins, carbohydrates, fiber, and nutrients. They are also extremely satisfying and have an added advantage in that they can be made in advance and reheated before serving. French *tians* and Italian *pasticcios* are creamy, with a béchamel base, while the Arab equivalents are often made with eggs. Serve them as main dishes, accompanied with salad. They are delicious both hot and cold and are perfect for buffet meals.

1 LARGE ONION, CHOPPED

1 1/2 TABLESPOONS OLIVE OIL

4 EGGS

1/2 CUP MILK

SALT AND FRESHLY GROUND WHITE
PEPPER TO TASTE

A PINCH OF NUTMEG

ABOUT 4 LARGE ZUCCHINI, VERY
THINLY SLICED

FOR THE SAUCE

1 TO 2 CLOVES GARLIC, FINELY
CHOPPED

1 TABLESPOON OLIVE OIL

ABOUT 6 MEDIUM TOMATOES,
PEELED AND CHOPPED

SALT AND PEPPER TO TASTE

1 TO 2 TEASPOONS SUGAR

1 TO 2 TABLESPOONS COARSELY
CHOPPED BLACK OLIVES

1 TO 2 TABLESPOONS CAPERS,
SQUEEZED TO REMOVE EXCESS
VINEGAR

ZUCCHINI FLAN WITH TOMATO SAUCE

The olives and capers in the sauce enhance the delicate flavors of the zucchini and creamy custard of this Provençal flan.

SERVES 4

Preheat the oven to 350° F.

Fry the onion in the oil over medium heat until very soft and golden, stirring often. Set aside to cool.

Beat the eggs lightly with a fork, then beat in the milk and add salt and white pepper and nutmeg. Add the fried onions and the zucchini and mix well.

Pour into a well-greased 10-inch flan mold or baking dish. Bake for 30 minutes, then cover the dish with foil and bake for 1 more hour until the flan is firm.

Meanwhile, prepare the sauce. Fry the garlic in the oil, stirring, until lightly colored. Add the tomatoes, salt, pepper, and sugar and simmer for 20 minutes until the sauce is thick. Add the olives and capers and cook for a few more minutes.

Serve the zucchini flan with the sauce poured over.

1 LARGE ONION, COARSELY
CHOPPED

2 TABLESPOONS SUNFLOWER OR
VEGETABLE OIL

1 1/2 POUNDS ZUCCHINI, CUT INTO
1/3-INCH SLICES

SALT

3 EGGS, LIGHTLY BEATEN

7 OUNCES MEDIUM GRATED
CHEDDAR CHEESE

FRESHLY GROUND WHITE PEPPER
TO TASTE

A PINCH NUTMEG

ZUCCHINI GRATIN

This is a dish from the Arab Mediterranean where it is often served with yoghurt. I have substituted Cheddar for the usual feta cheese because it complements the zucchini particularly well.

SERVES 4

Preheat the oven to 350° F.

Fry the onion in the oil over medium heat until golden. Set aside to cool.

Blanch the zucchini in boiling salted water for a few minutes (they should be slightly underdone) and drain. Mix the eggs with the fried onions and cheese, add white pepper and nutmeg, and fold in the zucchini.

Pour into a greased baking dish and bake for about 30 minutes until the eggs have set and the top is lightly browned.

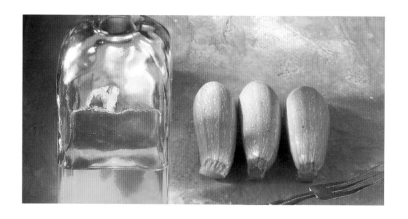

1 1/2 POUNDS EGGPLANTS, CUT INTO
1/3-INCH SLICES

SALT

1 LARGE ONION, CHOPPED

SUNFLOWER OIL FOR FRYING

1 1/2 POUNDS TOMATOES, PEELED
AND CHOPPED

PEPPER

2 TEASPOONS SUGAR

7 OUNCES FONTINA CHEESE,
THINLY SLICED

2 1/4 CUPS MILK

4 EGGS

2 TABLESPOONS FRESHLY GRATED
PARMIGIANO-REGGIANO

EGGPLANT, TOMATO, AND FONTINA FLAN

This *pasticcio di melanzane* hails from southern Italy.

SERVES 6

Soak the eggplants for 30 minutes in water with plenty of salt, then drain and pat dry with a cloth.

To make a tomato sauce, fry the onion in 2 tablespoons oil over medium heat until golden. Add the tomatoes, salt and pepper to taste, and sugar and simmer for 15 to 20 minutes.

Preheat the oven to 350° F.

Deep-fry the eggplant slices in hot oil very briefly, turning them over once, until slightly browned, then drain on paper towels. Alternatively, you can broil the slices: brush them generously with oil, arrange them on a baking sheet, and cook them under a hot broiler, turning to brown them on both sides.

In a baking dish, put layers of eggplant, Fontina, and tomato sauce.

Beat the milk with the eggs and Parmigiano, add salt and pepper to taste and pour over the dish.

Bake for 1¼ hours or until the eggs have set. Serve hot.

1 POUND EGGPLANTS, CUT INTO ROUND 1/3-INCH SLICES

SALT

VEGETABLE OR SUNFLOWER OIL FOR FRYING

PEPPER

4 TABLESPOONS CHOPPED FLAT-LEAF PARSLEY

1 RECIPE FRESH TOMATO SAUCE (SEE PAGE 218)

4 OUNCES FETA CHEESE, MASHED WITH A FORK

3 EGGS

VARIATIONS

For a *parmigiana di melanzane*, use a small bunch of torn basil leaves instead of the parsley, and top with 9 ounces diced fresh mozzarella cheese and 6 tablespoons freshly grated Parmigiano-Reggiano. Omit the eggs and feta.

A French version uses a béchamel sauce mixed with grated Gruyère as the topping.

BAKED EGGPLANTS WITH TOMATO SAUCE AND FETA

This is the Arab equivalent of the famous Italian *parmigiana di melanzane*.

SERVES 4

Preheat the oven to 400° F.

Sprinkle the eggplant with salt and leave for 30 minutes until the juices are drawn out. Then rinse off the salt and dry. Fry the slices very briefly in very hot oil (so that they absorb as little oil as possible), turning them over once, until browned. Drain on paper towels and arrange on the bottom of an 11-inch baking dish.

Sprinkle with salt and pepper to taste and the parsley and spoon the tomato sauce over the eggplants.

Beat the feta with the eggs until well blended and spoon the mixture over the tomato sauce.

Bake for 20 to 30 minutes until the eggs have set. Serve hot.

1 ½ POUNDS ORANGE PUMPKIN, PEELED AND CUT INTO PIECES

SALT AND FRESHLY GROUND WHITE PEPPER TO TASTE

A PINCH NUTMEG

1 SMALL ONION, CHOPPED

1 TABLESPOON BUTTER

1 TABLESPOON VEGETABLE OIL

1 TABLESPOON ALL-PURPOSE FLOUR

1 CUP MILK

2 EGGS, LIGHTLY BEATEN

2 TO 3 TABLESPOONS GRATED GRUYÈRE CHEESE

BAKED PUMPKIN CREAM

This creamy *tian de courge* of the Vaucluse in the south of France has a sweet, delicate flavor that everyone loves. It can be served as a first course or as a main dish if accompanied by Fresh Tomato Sauce (see page 218). You need the orange-fleshed pumpkin that you find in Indian, Greek, and Middle Eastern stores almost throughout the year. They are very large and are sold in slices with seeds and fibers removed.

SERVES 4

Preheat the oven to 400° F.

Put the pumpkin in a pan with about 4 tablespoons water over medium heat. Put the lid on and steam until very soft, about 15 minutes. Mash with a potato masher or fork, and add salt, white pepper, and nutmeg. Cook over medium heat, stirring for a few minutes, until most of the liquid has evaporated (pumpkin releases a lot of liquid).

Fry the onion in the butter and oil over medium heat until soft but not brown. Add the flour and cook, stirring, for 1 to 2 minutes.

Gradually add the milk, a little at a time, stirring to prevent lumps from forming, and cook over low heat until the white sauce thickens.

Mix the sauce with the pumpkin, add the eggs, and beat well. Pour into a well buttered 9-inch baking dish. Sprinkle with the cheese and bake for 40 minutes or until the top is slightly firm and golden.

1 1/2 POUNDS ORANGE PUMPKIN,
PEELED AND CUT INTO PIECES

2 EGGS, LIGHTLY BEATEN

4 OUNCES FETA CHEESE, MASHED

4 TABLESPOONS FRESHLY GRATED
PARMIGIANO-REGGIANO

PUMPKIN GRATIN

This recipe is from the eastern Mediterranean.

SERVES 4

Preheat the oven to 350° F.

Put the pumpkin in a pan with about 4 tablespoons water over medium heat. Put the lid on and steam until very soft, about 15 minutes. Mash with a potato masher or fork and cook over medium heat, stirring, for a few minutes until most of the liquid has evaporated (pumpkin releases a lot of liquid).

Beat the eggs together with the cheeses, then mix with the pumpkin. The cheeses are salty and you should not need to add extra salt, but taste to find out.

Pour into a greased 8-inch baking dish and bake for about 25 minutes or until firm.

14 OUNCES FRESH SPINACH OR FROZEN WHOLE LEAF SPINACH

1/2 ONION, CHOPPED

2 TABLESPOONS BUTTER

2 TABLESPOONS ALL-PURPOSE FLOUR

1 1/4 CUPS BOILING MILK

SALT AND PEPPER TO TASTE

A PINCH NUTMEG

2 EGGS, LIGHTLY BEATEN

2 HARD-BOILED EGGS, CUT INTO PIECES

2 OUNCES GRATED GRUYÈRE CHEESE

BAKED SPINACH WITH EGGS AND CHEESE

This *tian d'epinards*, a speciality of the Vaucluse, is a homely, satisfying dish.

SERVES 4

Preheat the oven to 400° F.

If using fresh spinach, wash and drain (remove the stems only if they are hard). Cook the spinach in a covered pan with no added water (the spinach steams in the water that clings to the leaves) until it crumples. Drain in a colander, reserving the juice. If using frozen spinach, defrost and press out and reserve the excess water.

In a pan, fry the onion in the butter over low heat until soft. Add the flour and stir. Gradually add the boiling milk and the reserved spinach juice and cook for 5 minutes, stirring constantly to prevent lumps from forming. Add salt and pepper, nutmeg, the eggs and spinach, and beat well.

Fold in the hard-boiled eggs and the cheese and pour into a greased 9-inch baking dish. Bake for 40 minutes or until the top is slightly firm and golden.

VARIATION

Use a mixture of sorrel or other greens with the spinach, and add a few pitted black olives.

VEGETABLE
SIDE DISHES

Anyone who has walked through a Mediterranean vegetable market knows how enthralling an experience it can be, with so much colorful fresh produce to choose from. Side dishes in Mediterranean countries are not the tasteless boiled or steamed vegetables we are used to here. They can be quite intriguing, yet simple at the same time. Serve them with egg dishes, flans and gratins, or with fish.

1 1/2 POUNDS BABY NEW POTATOES

2 WHOLE HEADS GARLIC, CUT IN
HALF CROSSWISE

3 BAY LEAVES

3 SPRIGS THYME

1 FRESH CHILI PEPPER

SALT AND PEPPER TO TASTE

EXTRA VIRGIN OLIVE OIL

HERBED NEW POTATOES

**In this traditional Provençal method of
cooking potatoes, they are boiled with garlic and
herbs and absorb the flavors through
their skins. I like to use the tiny new potatoes now
available in our supermarkets. Bring them
to the table with the halved garlic heads (which are
delicious spread on slices of fresh bread),
and the sprigs of thyme.**

SERVES 4

Rinse and scrub the potatoes. Put them in a pan over medium heat with enough water to cover and add the rest of the ingredients except the black pepper and the oil. Simmer until the potatoes are tender. Leave in the cooking water to absorb the flavors until you are ready to serve.

Drain and serve, hot or cold, with a drizzle of oil and a sprinkling of salt and pepper.

ABOUT 4 LARGE FLOURY POTATOES

SALT AND PEPPER

6 TABLESPOONS EXTRA VIRGIN
OLIVE OIL

4 TABLESPOONS CHOPPED FLAT-LEAF
PARSLEY

VARIATION

Add 3 tablespoons capers
or chopped pitted black
olives.

1 ONION, CHOPPED

2 TABLESPOONS EXTRA VIRGIN
OLIVE OIL

2 CLOVES GARLIC, CHOPPED

ABOUT 5 TO 6 TOMATOES, PEELED
AND CHOPPED

2 TEASPOONS SUGAR

SALT AND PEPPER

2 SPRIGS THYME, CHOPPED

1 1/2 POUNDS NEW POTATOES, CUT
INTO 3/4-INCH CUBES

ABOUT 3/4 CUP VEGETABLE STOCK

2 TABLESPOONS CHOPPED FLAT-LEAF
PARSLEY

MASHED POTATOES WITH OLIVE OIL AND PARSLEY

**This dish can be eaten hot or
at room temperature and goes well with fish.**

SERVES 4

Peel the potatoes and boil them in salted water until they are soft. Drain, reserving about ½ cup of the cooking water.

Mash the potatoes. Beat in the olive oil, add salt and pepper to taste and enough of the cooking water to achieve a soft, slightly moist texture. Stir in the parsley and serve hot.

POTATOES STEWED IN FRESH TOMATO SAUCE

I discovered this potato dish in Provence.

SERVES 4

Fry the onion in the oil over medium heat until golden. Add the garlic and cook, stirring, until the aroma rises.

Add the tomatoes, sugar, salt and pepper to taste, and thyme and simmer for about 15 minutes. Put in the potatoes with enough stock to cover and simmer gently until the potatoes are tender and the sauce is thick. Stir in the parsley and serve.

13 OUNCES FRESH SPINACH

2/3 CUP HEAVY CREAM

1 EGG

SALT AND PEPPER

SPINACH MOUSSE

**This wonderfully creamy French mousse can be
served with fish or as a first course
with Fresh Tomato Sauce (see page 218) and a
sprinkling of Parmigiano-Reggiano.**

SERVES 4

VARIATION

A quicker method—
resulting in an equally
delicious dish—is to fry
1 crushed garlic clove in
1 tablespoon sunflower oil,
add the cleaned spinach
leaves, and when they
soften, add heavy cream,
salt, pepper, and a pinch of
nutmeg. Serve hot.

Preheat the oven to 350° F.

Wash and drain the spinach and squeeze out the excess water. Remove the stems only if they are tough. Put the spinach in a pan over low heat and cook, covered, until they crumple into a soft mass. (The spinach will steam in the water that clings to the leaves.) Drain and squeeze out the juice, then blend the spinach to a paste in a food processor.

Add the cream, egg, and a little salt and pepper, and blend to a light homogenous cream.

Pour into a well-buttered, preferably nonstick, 8-inch mold or cake pan and bake for 30 minutes or until the top is slightly firm. Turn out onto a plate while still warm—it should come out easily.

NAVY BEANS

2¼ CUPS SMALL NAVY BEANS, SOAKED IN WATER FOR 2 HOURS

1 MEDIUM CARROT, CUT INTO 4 PIECES

1 MEDIUM ONION, QUARTERED

A FEW CELERY LEAVES

2 CLOVES GARLIC, PEELED

2 MEDIUM TOMATOES, PEELED AND CHOPPED

2 SPRIGS ROSEMARY

1 BAY LEAF

FRESHLY GROUND WHITE PEPPER

SALT

EXTRA VIRGIN OLIVE OIL

This is a good hot or cold accompaniment to egg dishes, flans and gratins, and fish. The vegetables and herbs lend delicious flavors.

SERVES 6

Drain the beans and put them in a pot with the rest of the ingredients except the salt and oil. Cover with water and simmer for 1 hour or until the beans and vegetables are tender, adding salt to taste toward the end.

Drain and serve hot or cold with a drizzle of olive oil.

SAUTÉED ZUCCHINI

ABOUT 3 TO 4 LARGE ZUCCHINI, CUT INTO THIN SLICES

4 TABLESPOONS MILD EXTRA VIRGIN OLIVE OIL OR SUNFLOWER OIL

1 CLOVE GARLIC, FINELY CHOPPED

SALT AND PEPPER

2 TEASPOONS DRIED MINT

JUICE OF ½ LEMON (OPTIONAL)

Zucchini sautéed in oil have a much better taste than boiled ones. These can be served hot, or at room temperature with lemon juice.

SERVES 4 TO 6

In a large skillet, sauté the zucchini in the oil with the garlic over medium heat. Season with salt and pepper to taste, turning the slices over a few times, until tender.

Add the mint toward the end, and the lemon juice, if using. Serve hot or at room temperature.

LEFT Navy Beans

1 CLOVE GARLIC, CRUSHED

4 TO 5 TABLESPOONS EXTRA VIRGIN OLIVE OIL

8 FROZEN ARTICHOKE HEARTS OR BOTTOMS, DEFROSTED AND SLICED

4 MEDIUM-SIZED NEW POTATOES, BOILED, PEELED, AND SLICED

SALT AND PEPPER

SAUTÉED ARTICHOKE HEARTS AND POTATOES

This is easy to make with frozen artichoke hearts (available from Middle Eastern Stores). It can be served as a first course.

SERVES 4

Fry the garlic in the oil over low heat for a few seconds, stirring. Add the artichokes and sauté, stirring, until tender. Add the potatoes, season to taste with salt and pepper, and cook, stirring, for a few minutes more until the potatoes are heated through. Serve hot.

14 OUNCES OKRA, PREFERABLY YOUNG AND SMALL

1 MEDIUM ONION, CUT IN HALF AND SLICED

3 TABLESPOONS VEGETABLE OR LIGHT EXTRA VIRGIN OLIVE OIL

2 CLOVES GARLIC, CHOPPED

4 MEDIUM TOMATOES, PEELED AND CHOPPED

SALT AND PEPPER

JUICE OF 1/2 LEMON

1 TO 2 TEASPOONS SUGAR, OR TO TASTE

1 SMALL BUNCH (1/4 CUP) FLAT-LEAF PARSLEY OR CILANTRO, CHOPPED

RIGHT Okra in Tomato Sauce

OKRA IN TOMATO SAUCE

Okra, or *bamia*, as it is called in Arabic, is a vegetable much loved in the eastern Mediterranean. But, unlike the eggplant, which the Turks claim to prepare in a hundred different ways, *bamia* is almost always cooked with onions and tomatoes. It is served hot with rice, or at room temperature as an appetizer.

SERVES 4

Trim the conical caps and wash and drain the okra.

Fry the onion in the oil over medium heat until golden. Add the garlic and stir for 1 to 2 minutes. Put in the okra and sauté, stirring, for about 5 minutes.

Add the tomatoes, salt and pepper to taste, lemon juice, and sugar and cook for 15 minutes. Stir in the parsley just before serving.

1 LARGE ONION, SLICED

3 TABLESPOONS PEANUT OR
VEGETABLE OIL

1 POUND PUMPKIN, CUT INTO
3/4-INCH CUBES

SALT AND PLENTY OF PEPPER

1 TEASPOON SUGAR, OR TO TASTE
(OPTIONAL)

1 TEASPOON CINNAMON

3 TABLESPOONS RAISINS

3 TABLESPOONS PINE NUTS

SAUTÉED PUMPKIN WITH RAISINS AND PINE NUTS

The raisin and pine nut partnership is something the Arabs brought to the Mediterranean region, all the way to Spain and Sicily. You find the garnish with spinach, rice, bulghur, and all kinds of dishes. It goes well with pumpkin in this North African dish, which provides a certain delicate sweetness to a vegetarian meal.

SERVES 4

In a large skillet, fry the onion in the oil over medium heat, stirring occasionally, until soft and golden.

Add the pumpkin and sauté over low heat for 5 minutes, turning the pieces over. Add salt, pepper, and sugar to taste, cinnamon, and raisins. Cover with a tight-fitting lid and cook for about 20 minutes or until the pumpkin is tender, turning the pumpkin over occasionally. It will release its own juices.

Dry-toast the pine nuts or fry them in just a film of oil in a skillet, shaking the pan to brown them evenly.

Serve the pumpkin hot or at room temperature, sprinkled with the pine nuts.

FISH AND SEAFOOD

Much of Mediterranean fish cookery is a matter of broiling, frying, roasting, or poaching, and marrying the fish with a dressing or sauce. Choose your fish and cook it by one of the methods on pages 150 to 163. Serve it with one of the marinades, dressings, or sauces on pages 144 to 150. Popular Mediterranean fish include sea bass, sea bream, sole, gurnard, John Dory, red mullet, hake, and tuna. Most of them are easy to obtain, but you can substitute fish from other seas, such as cod, haddock, halibut, snapper, and catfish.

JUICE OF 1 LEMON

6 TABLESPOONS EXTRA VIRGIN
OLIVE OIL

SALT AND PEPPER TO TASTE

3 TABLESPOONS FINELY CHOPPED
FLAT-LEAF PARSLEY

OIL AND LEMON DRESSING

**This is the standard, all-purpose
Mediterranean dressing for fish.**

SERVES 4

Mix the ingredients cold and pour over the fish.

1/2 CUP MILD EXTRA VIRGIN OLIVE
OIL

JUICE OF 1/2 LEMON

4 MEDIUM TOMATOES, PEELED AND
DICED

SALT AND PEPPER TO TASTE

1 TO 1 1/2 TEASPOONS SUGAR

WARM LEMON AND
TOMATO DRESSING

**This is particularly delicious with
grilled or broiled fish.**

SERVES 4

Heat the oil over low heat with the lemon juice and
tomatoes until the tomatoes are heated through.
Remove from the heat and add salt, pepper, and sugar.

---

3 MEDIUM TOMATOES

1/2 TO 1 SMALL RED CHILI

1 CLOVE GARLIC, CRUSHED

1-INCH PIECE GINGER, GRATED (OR
USE THE JUICE, PRESSED OUT USING
A GARLIC PRESS)

1/2 RED ONION, FINELY CHOPPED

JUICE OF 1/2 LIME OR LEMON

4 TABLESPOONS EXTRA VIRGIN
OLIVE OIL

SALT AND PEPPER TO TASTE

1 TEASPOON SUGAR

SAUCE VIERGE

**This spicy raw tomato sauce goes well with raw
marinated fish and with cold fish.**

SERVES 4

Skin and finely chop the tomatoes, and finely chop the
chili. Mix with the rest of the ingredients and adjust the
seasoning to taste.

1 LARGE BUNCH (²/3 CUP)
CILANTRO, CHOPPED

4 CLOVES GARLIC, CRUSHED

1 TEASPOON GROUND CUMIN

1 TEASPOON PAPRIKA

¹/4 TO ¹/2 TEASPOON CHILI POWDER
(OPTIONAL)

6 TABLESPOONS PEANUT OR MILD
EXTRA VIRGIN OLIVE OIL

JUICE OF 1 LEMON OR
3 TABLESPOONS WHITE WINE
VINEGAR

CHERMOULA

**This hot, spicy, garlicky mixture is
the ubiquitous Moroccan sauce for fish. It
goes on every kind of fish—fried,
grilled, broiled, baked, and stewed. Use
half the quantity to marinate the fish
for 30 minutes before cooking, and pour the
rest on as a sauce just before serving.**

SERVES 4

Blend everything together in the food processor.

2 HEADS GARLIC, PREFERABLY
YOUNG, WITH LARGE CLOVES

1 CUP DRY WHITE WINE

2 TABLESPOONS EXTRA VIRGIN
OLIVE OIL

SALT AND PEPPER

GARLIC PURÉE

**Cooks in Provence have many ways of
turning garlic into something mild and delicate.
This *purée d'ail*, in which garlic is simmered
in white wine, is delicious with all kinds of fish.
I have tried it with pan-fried fillet of
whiting and also with broiled bream. Spread it
on just before serving.**

SERVES 4 TO 6

Peel the garlic cloves and boil them in the wine for 15
to 20 minutes or until very soft. Drain and mash to a
purée with a fork, then stir in the oil and a little salt
and pepper.

1 VERY LARGE BUNCH (2 CUPS) FLAT-LEAF PARSLEY, STEMS REMOVED

1/2 CUP PINE NUTS

5 SMALL GHERKINS

8 PITTED GREEN OLIVES

3 CLOVES GARLIC, CRUSHED

3 TABLESPOONS WHITE WINE VINEGAR OR THE JUICE OF 1/2 LEMON

SALT AND PEPPER TO TASTE

ABOUT 1 CUP MILD EXTRA VIRGIN OLIVE OIL

SALSA VERDE

This Italian herb sauce is a good accompaniment to marinated and cold poached fish. The sauce keeps well in a jar with a layer of oil at the top.

SERVES 6

Blend all the ingredients except the oil in a food processor, then add the oil gradually—enough to achieve a light paste.

---

1 SLICE WHITE BREAD, CRUSTS REMOVED

1 1/4 CUPS PINE NUTS

JUICE OF 1 TO 2 LEMONS, OR TO TASTE

1 TO 2 CLOVES GARLIC, CRUSHED

SALT AND FRESHLY GROUND WHITE PEPPER

1/2 CUP VEGETABLE OIL

TARATOR

This lemony pine nut sauce is often seen on grand Arab buffet tables spread all over a large skinned, boned and reshaped poached fish.

SERVES 6

Soak the bread in water and squeeze dry. Put it in a food processor with the pine nuts, lemon juice, and garlic, a little salt and white pepper to taste, and purée, adding enough oil to achieve a mixture with the consistency of mayonnaise.

RIGHT Halibut Poached in White Wine (see page 160) with Salsa Verde

2 RED BELL PEPPERS

ABOUT 6 MEDIUM TOMATOES

1 LARGE SLICE WHITE BREAD,
CRUSTS REMOVED

5 TABLESPOONS EXTRA VIRGIN
OLIVE OIL

3 CLOVES GARLIC, CRUSHED

3/4 CUP BLANCHED ALMONDS

JUICE OF 1/2 LEMON, OR MORE TO
TASTE

1/2 RED CHILI PEPPER

SALT AND PEPPER

VARIATION

Blanched hazelnuts or
a mixture of almonds and
hazelnuts can be used
instead of the almonds.

ROMESCO

**I love this roast pepper and almond sauce.
It is an approximation of the famous Spanish sauce
based on the dark, wine-colored *ñora* peppers,
which are sweet and slightly hot. The rich, nutty,
piquant flavor makes it a delightful accompaniment
to vegetables as well as fish. It keeps well in a jar
with a film of olive oil at the top. Serve it with
grilled, broiled, steamed, or fried fish and seafood,
or with fish stews and soups.**

SERVES 12

Roast the peppers (see page 216) and tomatoes under the broiler. Peel them and seed the peppers.

Fry the bread in 2 tablespoons of the oil over medium heat until golden, turning it over once. Add the garlic and cook, stirring, until it just begins to color.

Toast the almonds in a dry skillet, shaking the pan to brown them all over.

In a food processor, blend the bread, garlic, almonds, the remaining oil, lemon juice, and chili to a paste. Add the peppers, tomatoes, and salt and pepper to taste, and purée until the mixture is smooth.

Serve in a bowl and pass it around for people to help themselves.

*RIGHT Grilled Tuna (see page 157)
with Romesco*

2 MEDIUM ONIONS, CUT IN HALF AND SLICED

2 TABLESPOONS EXTRA VIRGIN OLIVE OIL

2 BAY LEAVES

1 SPRIG THYME

1 SPRIG ROSEMARY

1 TABLESPOON HONEY

1 TEASPOON WHITE WINE VINEGAR

SALT AND PLENTY OF PEPPER

ONION FONDUE WITH HONEY

**Use this to accompany and also to stuff a fish.
I stuffed a large bream with it.
The fishmonger had removed the backbones for
me through the backs and I stuffed it
easily and roasted it. Because the fondue (the
onions are melting soft, hence the name) is
sweet, it is best to use a tart dressing of oil and
lemon on the fish to cut the sweetness.**

SERVES 4

In a covered pan, cook the onion in the oil with the bay leaves, thyme, and rosemary over very low heat for about 30 minutes, stirring occasionally, until the onion is very soft and just beginning to color. It will stew in its juice rather than fry.

Add the honey, vinegar, and salt and pepper to taste and cook for another 10 minutes over medium heat, or until much of the liquid has evaporated.

STUFFED FISH

SERVES 4

Ask the fishmonger to scale and clean a bream or sea bass weighing about 3 pounds and to remove the backbones through the back. Alternatively, have the fish filleted with the head left on one of the fillets. Brush the fish with 2 to 3 tablespoons extra virgin olive oil and season lightly inside and out with salt and pepper. Stuff with Onion Fondue with Honey or Garlic Purée (page

145) and place in a baking dish. Pour on the juice of ½ lemon or about 4 tablespoons dry white wine. Put under the broiler for 5 to 6 minutes until the skin is crisp and brown, then bake in a preheated 375° F. oven for 25 minutes or until the flesh flakes easily away from the bone when you cut it with a pointed knife.

ROASTED FISH

**Any large fish is suitable for this recipe.
Sea bass is the grandest fish of the Mediterranean,
but a large bream (daurade) is marvelous too.**

SERVES 8

1 SEA BASS OR BREAM WEIGHING ABOUT 5 POUNDS

6 TABLESPOONS LIGHT EXTRA VIRGIN OLIVE OIL

SALT AND PEPPER

JUICE OF 1 LEMON

6 TABLESPOONS DRY WHITE WINE

Preheat the oven to 375° F.

Brush the fish with 1 to 2 tablespoons of the oil and season lightly inside and out with salt and pepper.

Place in a baking dish with a mixture of the lemon juice, the remaining oil, and the white wine.

Put under the broiler for 5 to 6 minutes until the skin is crisp and brown, then bake for about 35 minutes or until the flesh flakes easily away from the bone when you cut it with a pointed knife.

VARIATIONS

A Moroccan variation is to marinate the fish for 30 minutes in the following mixture, blended in a food processor: 1 bunch (½ cup) cilantro, 1 bunch (½ cup) flat-leaf parsley, 3 crushed garlic cloves, salt, 6 tablespoons extra virgin olive oil, ½ to 1 teaspoon ground ginger, and ¼ to ½ teaspoon saffron powder.

RIGHT Roast Bream Stuffed with
Onion Fondue with Honey
(page 150)

2 SALMON FILLETS, ABOUT 2 POUNDS TOTAL

3 TABLESPOONS COARSE SEA SALT

3/4 CUP MILD EXTRA VIRGIN OLIVE OIL

JUICE OF 1 LEMON

1 LARGE BUNCH (ABOUT 1/2 CUP) MIXED HERBS INCLUDING CHERVIL, CHIVES, AND DILL, CHOPPED

MARINATED FISH

Fish lightly cured in salt and marinated in olive oil, lemon juice, and herbs is a tradition in the Mediterranean. Start the night before you plan to serve. The important thing is to get very fresh fish. Ask the fishmonger to fillet a salmon but to leave the skin on.

SERVES 10

Carefully remove any small bones from the fillets (tweezers will help). Sprinkle the fillets with the salt, on the skin side as well as inside.

Put the fillets together to reform the fish and place in a large deep dish. Cover with plastic wrap and leave in the refrigerator for about 12 hours, turning the salmon over when the juices start to collect.

Scrape off the salt with a spatula and wipe the fish with paper towels, then rinse the fish in cold running water. Taste a piece. If it is too salty, soak it in fresh water for as long as it takes to get rid of the saltiness.

Mix together the oil, lemon juice, and herbs and pour into 1 or 2 large dishes. Lay the fillets, flesh side down, on the marinade and refrigerate, covered with plastic wrap, for at least 3 hours (the fillets can be left in the marinade for several hours).

Before serving, cut diagonal slices across the grain of the fish—they can be very thin or fairly thick. It is lovely served with the raw tomato sauce, Sauce Vierge (see page 144).

VARIATION

The fish is also delicious marinated in the herbs and olive oil alone, with no lemon.

Serve with a sauce: Salsa Verde (see page 146); Aïoli (see page 220); Tarator (see page 146); or Sauce Vierge (see page 144).

TIP

Do not use fine salt as it penetrates the fish and makes it too salty, instead of drawing out the juices.

PAN-COOKED FISH FILLET

Cooking filleted fish in a large heavy skillet or Spanish *plancha*, or a heavy griddle, barely filmed with oil, is currently the most popular way in France. It is also the easiest. The French call it *poêlé*. It is fashionable to cook the fillet on the skin side only, resulting in a wonderfully moist, juicy texture. You can use any fish fillet, large or small, but it must have the skin on. Sea bass fillets and whole sides of salmon cook beautifully in this way. Scoring the thick part on the skin side prevents curling and allows the fish to cook evenly.

Oil the skillet or griddle and heat it to just below the smoking point. Brush the fish with oil and sprinkle with salt. Place it skin side down in the pan and cook, uncovered, over medium heat. It will gradually cook through to the top. The fish is done when it is opaque all the way through and the flesh flakes easily. When cooking a thin fillet, the heat can be quite high. A thick piece is best done over lower heat; a thick salmon fillet can take more than 20 minutes. Some people like to finish by putting the fish, brushed with oil, under the broiler for a few seconds.

If you do not have a very large skillet or *plancha*, cut the fillets into manageable pieces (escalopes).

Serve sprinkled with parsley and accompanied with a sauce such as Salsa Verde (see page 146), Romesco (see page 148), Aïoli (see page 220), Tarator (see page 146), Sauce Vierge (see page 144), or Onion Fondue with Honey (see page 150).

GRILLED FISH

For fish steaks, use tuna, swordfish, hake, turbot, cod, haddock, or halibut. Simply brush the fish with olive oil and sprinkle with salt and pepper. Place the fish about 2 inches from the fire, on a well-oiled grill over glowing embers, or under the broiler. Cook for 2 to 4 minutes on each side. The fish is done when the flesh flakes away from the bone when you cut with the point of a knife. It is important not to overcook. The best way to cook tuna is to sear it on the outside at high heat (close to the fire) and to leave it rare inside.

For whole fish, use small or medium-sized bream, gurnard, red mullet, sardines, and also flat fish such as sole and skate. Have them scaled and cleaned but keep the heads on. Brush with extra virgin oil and season with salt and pepper. Cook for 2 to 5 minutes on each side, depending on the size. Cut into one fish with a pointed knife to see if they are done.

For fish fillet (large fish split along the backbone), use sea bass, bream, hake, swordfish, turbot, or salmon. Leave the skin on. Brush with extra virgin olive oil and season with salt and pepper. Cook on the skin side only, not too close to the fire and do not turn over or the fish will dry out. It does cook through.

Serve grilled fish with a dressing or sauce. Dress with Oil and Lemon Dressing (see page 144), adding, if desired, chopped herbs such as fennel, thyme, marjoram, oregano, or tarragon; or try Warm Lemon and Tomato Dressing (see page 144).

Accompany with any of the sauces on pages 144 through 150 and lemon wedges.

DEEP-FRIED FISH

Deep-frying is the most popular way of cooking fish in the Arab world. The method was introduced by the Arabs in the early Middle Ages to Spain and Sicily. Southern Italians excel at their *fritti misti*—a medley that may include red mullet, sardines, anchovies, whitebait, fillet of sole, baby hake, baby squid, and large shrimp. The Andalusians are the world's best at frying any kind of fish and seafood. Many people these days are averse to this method of cooking, but the result is delightful and worth trying.

To ensure success you must follow these rules:

- Use olive oil to fry because it can reach high temperatures without deteriorating (it can be filtered and reused). There must be enough oil to cover the fish and the temperature should remain constant. Always start frying at high heat to seal the fish, then turn the heat down to moderate if necessary.

- Use a large, deep pan so that there is no risk of the oil bubbling over.

- Fry fish of about the same size at the same time.

- Season the fish with salt inside and out and dredge lightly but thoroughly in flour.

- Small fish must be fried very quickly at a very high heat so that they are crisp and brown but still moist inside.

- Larger fish take longer (3 to 4 minutes on each side) and need a lower temperature so they have time to cook inside before the skin burns.

- Fish steaks and fillets are best first dipped in seasoned flour then in lightly beaten egg for extra protection.

- When frying, turn only once, lift out and drain on paper towels.

- Shrimp, squid, and large mussels are usually dipped in batter before frying. To make a batter for 1 pound seafood to serve 4 people, combine ¾ cup flour with 1 teaspoon baking powder, ½ teaspoon salt, 2 tablespoons olive oil, and ⅔ cup water. Beat well and let it rest for 30 minutes.

⅔ CUP DRY WHITE WINE

⅔ CUP WATER

2 BAY LEAVES

A FEW PARSLEY SPRIGS

SALT AND WHITE PEPPER TO TASTE

A PINCH OF SAFFRON (OPTIONAL)

4 FISH STEAKS OR FILLETS

VARIATION

This is a simple and marvelous Italian preparation: fry 1 chopped garlic clove in 4 tablespoons extra virgin olive oil over low heat. Add ⅔ cup dry white wine and 2 chopped tomatoes. Bring to a boil and add the fish fillets. Simmer for 5 minutes. Add 1 tablespoon chopped flat-leaf parsley and serve in a soup bowl with the sauce.

POACHED FISH IN WHITE WINE

Poached fish—fillets or steaks—are good to serve hot or cold. You may use any white fish. The saffron in the poaching liquid is not usual but it is sometimes added.

SERVES 4

Put all the ingredients except the fish in a pan wide enough to contain the fish in one layer. Bring to a boil and lower the heat to a simmer.

Add the fish and simmer gently for 3 to 6 minutes, depending on the thickness and type of fish, until the flesh is opaque and flakes when you cut it with the point of a knife.

Serve with Oil and Lemon Dressing (see page 144). Accompany with Salsa Verde (see page 146), Sauce Vierge (see page 144), Garlic Purée (see page 145), Mayonnaise or Aïoli (see page 220), or Tarator (see page 146).

4 PIECES FISH FILLET

2 TABLESPOONS BUTTER

1 TABLESPOON SUNFLOWER OR
VEGETABLE OIL

SALT AND PEPPER

AROMATICS (SEE BELOW)

SAUTÉED FISH

This is the quickest and easiest way to cook fish fillets. Another advantage is that you can easily incorporate herbs and aromatics.

SERVES 4

Sauté the fish in a mixture of sizzling butter and oil, adding salt and pepper and aromatics, for about 5 minutes or until the flesh is opaque and begins to flake. Turn the fillets over once.

AROMATICS

For a Moroccan flavor, add ⅓ teaspoon powdered ginger and ¼ teaspoon saffron to the pan with the butter and oil.

For a different North African flavor, add 1 teaspoon ground cumin, 1 teaspoon paprika, ¼ teaspoon cayenne, the juice of ½ lemon and a large bunch (½ cup) chopped cilantro.

For a touch of southern France, add 2 to 3 tablespoons chopped fennel leaves and 1 tablespoon pastis.

For another Moroccan fish variation, add ½ to 1 Preserved Lemon Peel (see page 219), rinsed and cut into small pieces; 8 to 12 pitted green olives; and 2 tablespoons capers.

2 (1-POUND) PACKETS BOUGHT
FROZEN PUFF PASTRY, DEFROSTED

1 EGG, SEPARATED

5 POUNDS SALMON OR SEA BASS
FILLETS

3 TABLESPOONS SUNFLOWER OR
VEGETABLE OIL

JUICE OF 1/2 LEMON

SALT AND FRESHLY GROUND WHITE
PEPPER

FISH COOKED IN PASTRY

**Salmon in pastry has long been a favorite
party dish. In France, sea bass is used for grand
occasions. The following is a Mediterranean
version of a *poisson en croûte*. Ask the fishmonger
to fillet and skin the fish for you.**

SERVES 8 TO 10

Preheat the oven to 450° F.

The puff pastry packets are divided into 2 pieces of
dough, each weighing 8 ounces. Stick 2 pieces from one
packet together and roll out. Cut it in the shape of the
fish but slightly larger, adding a tail. As a rough guide,
the dough should be about the thickness of a coin.

Lay it on a damp baking sheet and leave it in a cold
place to rest for 15 minutes. Brush it with egg white to
prevent it from getting too soggy with the fish juices, and
prick it all over with a fork so that it does not puff up
unevenly.

Bake it for 8 minutes or until crisp and lightly
colored. Turn it over, brush the other side with egg white,
return it to the oven, and bake for a few more minutes
until the second side is golden. Let it cool.

Brush the fish fillets with the oil and lemon juice
and sprinkle lightly with salt and pepper. Place them on
the baked pastry.

Roll out the remaining pieces of dough to the
thickness of a coin, sticking them together to make one
large sheet, that will cover the fish.

Cover the fish entirely with the dough, and cut around it, leaving a margin of about 1 inch, including around the tail.

Using a rounded knife, lift the edge of the baked pastry base and tuck the dough margin underneath, pressing gently to seal.

Decorate the pastry. Using a teaspoon, make a scale design on the body. Using the leftover scraps of dough, attach thin ribbons to represent the tail, gills and fins and use a little ball for the eye.

Brush all over with egg yolk and bake for 15 minutes until puffed up and golden. Then lower the heat to 300° F. and bake for another 30 minutes.

If the pastry seems to brown too quickly, cover it with foil or with slightly damp parchment paper.

Serve accompanied with Fresh Tomato Sauce (see page 218), adding the ginger, or with Warm Lemon and Tomato Dressing (see see page 144).

4 RED MULLET, WEIGHING ABOUT
2 POUNDS TOTAL

4 CLOVES GARLIC, CHOPPED

4 TABLESPOONS MILD EXTRA VIRGIN
OLIVE OIL

ABOUT 6 RIPE TOMATOES, PEELED
AND CHOPPED

SALT AND PEPPER

1 1/2 TEASPOONS SUGAR

4 LEMON SLICES

12 BLACK OLIVES, PITTED
(OPTIONAL)

3 TABLESPOONS CHOPPED FLAT-LEAF
PARSLEY

RED MULLET IN TOMATO SAUCE

This dish looks beautiful, red on red.

SERVES 4

Have the fish scaled and cleaned with the heads left on.

In a large skillet that can hold the fish in one layer, fry the garlic in the oil over medium heat until it just begins to color. Add the tomatoes, salt and pepper to taste, sugar, and the lemon slices and simmer for 10 minutes, then put in the fish and the olives, if using, and simmer for 4 minutes or until the fish flakes easily away from the bone. Add the parsley just before serving.

$4^{1}/_{2}$ CUPS MILK

$1^{1}/_{2}$ TABLESPOONS TOMATO PASTE

$^{1}/_{4}$ TEASPOON SAFFRON

8 EGGS

SALT AND FRESHLY GROUND WHITE
PEPPER

BUTTER

$1^{1}/_{2}$ POUNDS POTATOES, PEELED
AND THINLY SLICED

3 POUNDS FISH FILLETS, CUT INTO
$1^{3}/_{4}$-INCH PIECES

FOR THE SAUCE

4 TO 5 CLOVES GARLIC

$^{1}/_{2}$ TO 1 RED CHILI PEPPER, FINELY
CHOPPED OR 1 LARGE PINCH
CAYENNE

2 TABLESPOONS OLIVE OIL

2 (14-OUNCE) CANS ITALIAN
CRUSHED TOMATOES

SALT

1 TO 2 TEASPOONS SUGAR

CREAMY FISH FLAN
WITH SPICY TOMATO SAUCE

**This fish dish—a delicately flavored creamy
flan served with a hot peppery sauce—
is from Provence. You can use one type of fish
only or a variety of firm white fish such
as cod and haddock, as well as salmon. Buy fish
fillets and have them skinned.**

SERVES 8

Preheat the oven to 350° F.

In a saucepan over medium heat, bring the milk to
a boil. Dilute the tomato paste in a little of the milk and
add it to the pan with the saffron.

Beat the eggs in a bowl then gradually beat in the
hot milk. Add salt and white pepper to taste.

Grease a 14-inch baking dish with butter. Arrange
a layer of potatoes at the bottom, then add a layer of fish
and sprinkle lightly with salt. Pour the milk and egg
mixture over the top.

Place the dish in an oven tray and pour water into
the tray up to the level of the custard, so that the flan
cooks *au bain-marie*. Bake for 1 to $1^{1}/_{4}$ hours or until the
custard sets.

Meanwhile, make the sauce. Fry the garlic with the
chili pepper in the oil over medium heat until the aroma
rises. Add the tomatoes, salt and sugar to taste, and cook
for 10 minutes.

Serve the flan hot with the sauce on the side.

FISH COUSCOUS WITH QUINCE

FOR THE COUSCOUS

2¹/₂ CUPS MEDIUM-GROUND COUSCOUS

2¹/₂ CUPS WARM WATER

¹/₂ TO 1 TEASPOON SALT

3 TO 4 TABLESPOONS PEANUT OR LIGHT VEGETABLE OIL

FOR THE FISH

4 TO 5 CLOVES GARLIC, CHOPPED

3 TABLESPOONS PEANUT OR VEGETABLE OIL

2 POUNDS PLUM TOMATOES, PEELED AND CHOPPED

SALT

2 TEASPOONS SUGAR

1 TO 2 CHILIES, CUT IN HALF LENGTHWISE AND SEEDED

1-INCH PIECE GINGER, PEELED AND DICED

2 LARGE QUINCES

2 POUNDS FISH FILLET, SKINNED

This was inspired by two Moroccan dishes—a fish couscous with quince, raisins, and chick peas; and a tomato and quince sauce. Use skinned fillets of a firm white fish such as cod, haddock, or whiting.

SERVES 8

Preheat the oven to 400° F.

Soak and prepare the couscous in a baking dish according to the directions on pages 93 to 94, cover with foil, and set aside.

Fry the garlic in the oil over medium heat until it just begins to color. Add the tomatoes, salt to taste, sugar, and chilies and simmer over low heat. Crush the ginger pieces in a garlic press over the pan to extract the juice. Discard the pressed ginger.

Peel, core, and slice the quinces and immediately add them to the pan so that they do not turn brown.

Cook, covered, for 30 minutes or until the quinces are tender. The time varies depending on the size, quality, and ripeness of the fruit. Remove one or both of the chilies when you think the sauce is spicy enough.

Meanwhile, finish heating the couscous in the oven. About 20 minutes before serving, put the couscous, still covered with foil, in the oven to heat through.

About 5 to 10 minutes before serving, add the fish to the sauce. Simmer until the flesh flakes easily. Serve in soup plates, the couscous first and the stew on top.

TIP

Quinces are a very hard fruit and you will need a large strong knife to cut them.

4 CLOVES GARLIC, CRUSHED

1 1/2 TEASPOONS GROUND CUMIN

SALT

ABOUT 1/2 CUP OLIVE OIL

4 SMALL WINGS OF SKATE
WEIGHING 2 POUNDS TOTAL

ABOUT 4 TO 5 NEW POTATOES,
BOILED AND SLICED

PEPPER

2 TABLESPOONS CAPERS

1 LEMON, QUARTERED

SKATE WITH CUMIN AND POTATOES

All over North Africa, cumin is the standard flavoring for fish. Small skate, tender enough to fry quickly, should be used for this Tunisian dish. The wings are bought already dressed from the fishmonger.

SERVES 4

Mix together the garlic, cumin, salt to taste, and 3 to 4 tablespoons of the oil. Cut the fish into pieces about 2 inches wide, cutting in between the long soft bones, and rub the pieces with the garlic mixture.

In a large skillet, fry the fish pieces in batches in shallow oil over medium heat, about 4 minutes on each side, until the flesh flakes easily away from the bone. Transfer the fish to a baking dish, cover with foil, and keep warm in the oven.

Sauté the potatoes slowly in the same oil, adding salt and pepper to taste and more oil, turning occasionally, until they are light golden. Add the capers to the potatoes toward the end.

Serve the fish hot on a bed of the sautéed potatoes, accompanied with lemon wedges.

VARIATION

Large pieces of skate can be used but they must first be boiled for about 10 minutes.

2 CLOVES GARLIC, CHOPPED

4 1/2 OUNCES PEELED, COOKED KING PRAWNS, OR ABOUT 10 UNCOOKED, PEELED PRAWNS

2 TABLESPOONS OLIVE OIL

SALT AND PEPPER

1 1/2 TEASPOONS TOMATO PASTE

3 TABLESPOONS COGNAC

SAUTÉED PRAWNS WITH COGNAC

Cooked king prawns are common in supermarkets now, but if you can find uncooked, fresh or frozen ones, they are even better. This makes a luxurious dish for two. Large uncooked prawns need shelling and deveining. To do this, remove the black thread that runs the length of the prawn.

SERVES 2

Sauté the garlic and the prawns in the oil over high heat, stirring, until the precooked prawns are heated through or until the uncooked ones turn pink. Add salt and pepper to taste, tomato paste, and cognac and cook for 30 seconds. To serve, you can ignite the cognac and flambée the sauce.

4 1/2 POUNDS MUSSELS

2 CLOVES GARLIC, FINELY CHOPPED
OR CRUSHED

2 TABLESPOONS EXTRA VIRGIN
OLIVE OIL

2 1/4 CUPS DRY WHITE WINE

PEPPER

A HANDFUL OF FLAT-LEAF PARSLEY,
CHOPPED

MUSSELS WITH GARLIC AND WHITE WINE

I have been to restaurants in Paris that specialize in mussels and serve them in thirty different ways, but the classic and simple *moules à la marinière* is how people still choose to make them at home in the south of France.

SERVES 4 TO 6

Clean the mussels (see page 216).

In a very large pan, fry the garlic in the oil over medium heat until it just begins to color. Add the wine and boil for 5 minutes.

Add the mussels and plenty of pepper. Cover the pan and cook over low heat for about 2 minutes—until the mussels open. Immediately remove from the heat.

Discard the mussels that did not open. Use a slotted spoon to transfer the mussels to serving bowls or soup plates. Strain the winey mussel broth through a fine cheesecloth or strainer and pour a little into each bowl. Sprinkle with parsley.

1 POUND SMALL SQUID

2 CLOVES GARLIC, CHOPPED

1 RED CHILI, SEEDED AND MINCED

3 TABLESPOONS OLIVE OIL

SALT AND PEPPER

1 TABLESPOON LEMON JUICE

1 TABLESPOON CHOPPED FLAT-LEAF
PARSLEY

1 LEMON, CUT INTO WEDGES

BABY SQUID WITH GARLIC AND CHILIES

SERVES 4

Clean the squid and cut the body pouches into rings (see page 216).

Sauté the garlic and chili lightly in the oil over low heat. When the garlic begins to color, add the squid and raise the heat to high. Season with salt and pepper to taste and sauté briefly over medium heat, turning over the pieces, for 2 to 3 minutes only. Sprinkle with lemon juice and parsley and serve at once, accompanied with the lemon wedges.

3 CLOVES GARLIC, FINELY CHOPPED

3 TABLESPOONS EXTRA VIRGIN
OLIVE OIL

1 HOT RED CHILI, SEEDED AND
MINCED, OR 1 VERY LARGE PINCH
CHILI POWDER (OPTIONAL)

6 MEDIUM RIPE TOMATOES, PEELED
AND CHOPPED

1 CUP DRY WHITE WINE

SALT AND PEPPER

1 TO 2 TEASPOONS SUGAR, OR TO
TASTE

14 OUNCES SPAGHETTINI,
TAGLIOLINI, OR TAGLIATELLE

1 POUND FLESHY SHELLED COOKED
SHRIMP

4 TABLESPOONS FINELY CHOPPED
FLAT-LEAF PARSLEY

VARIATIONS

Make the sauce without
tomatoes and add about
¾ cup heavy cream at the
end.

For a mixed seafood pasta
use 1½ pounds mussels,
9 ounces small squid,
and 7 ounces shrimp.

PASTA WITH SHRIMP

**Some years ago the *Sunday Telegraph*
asked me to do a piece on the favorite dishes
of famous Italians, including Luciano
Pavarotti, Claudio Abbado, Armani, and Valentino.
Most of them said that their favorite food was the
seafood pasta they made themselves. One or
two used unorthodox ingredients such as
champagne or a little curry and cream,
but most were purists, preferring the classic
dishes with shrimp or mussels.**

SERVES 4

Fry the garlic in the oil over medium heat until it just
begins to color. Add the chili and tomatoes and cook for
5 minutes.

Add the wine. Season with salt and pepper to taste,
add sugar, and simmer for 10 minutes to reduce the
sauce.

Meanwhile, cook the pasta in plenty of boiling
salted water until *al dente* and drain in a colander.

Add the shrimp to
the sauce and heat
through when the pasta
is ready; stir in the
parsley. Pour the sauce
over the pasta and serve.

2 POUNDS MUSSELS

SALT

3/4 CUP DRY WHITE WINE

14 OUNCES SPAGHETTI OR
LINGUINE

2 TO 4 CLOVES GARLIC, CHOPPED

6 TO 8 TABLESPOONS EXTRA VIRGIN
OLIVE OIL

PEPPER

5 TABLESPOONS CHOPPED FLAT-LEAF
PARSLEY

SPAGHETTI WITH MUSSELS IN WHITE WINE

Clams are often used rather than mussels, but mussels make sense because they are more fleshy. Here they are *in bianco*, that is, without tomatoes, which best preserves the pure flavor of the sea. Linguine may be used instead of spaghetti. Do not serve grated cheese with this dish.

SERVES 4

Clean and prepare the mussels (see page 216). Place a large pot of lightly salted water over high heat to boil. Put the mussels in a large pan with half the wine. Cover and cook over high heat for about 1 minute. Remove from the heat as soon as the mussels open. Discard any that remain closed. Strain the juices from the pan and reserve. Keep the mussels warm in the oven.

Cook the spaghetti in the water until *al dente*.

Meanwhile, heat the garlic in 1 tablespoon of the oil over medium heat until it begins to color and the aroma rises. Add the mussel juice, plenty of pepper, and the rest of the wine and oil and raise the heat to high. Boil vigorously for a few minutes to reduce the sauce.

Drain the spaghetti as soon as it is *al dente*. Mix well with the sauce, sprinkle with the parsley and serve with the mussels on top. Or you may mix the drained spaghetti in the pan with the mussels before serving.

6 TABLESPOONS MILD EXTRA VIRGIN OLIVE OIL

2 TABLESPOONS BALSAMIC VINEGAR

SALT AND PEPPER TO TASTE

1/2 QUANTITY MIXED GREEN LEAF AND HERB SALAD (PAGE 16)

8 SCALLOPS

1 TABLESPOON LIGHT VEGETABLE OR EXTRA VIRGIN OLIVE OIL

SCALLOPS WITH BALSAMIC VINEGAR DRESSING

The secret of cooking scallops is to cook them as briefly as possible. They make a royal first course, served on a bed of Mixed Green Leaf and Herb Salad, using the dressing in this recipe.

SERVES 2

To make the dressing, mix together 6 tablespoons olive oil, vinegar, and salt and pepper. Use half to dress the green salad.

Wash the scallops and pull away the intestinal thread. Briefly sear them in an oiled skillet over high heat for 30 to 40 seconds on each side. Serve hot on a bed of the dressed salad with a drizzle of dressing.

RIGHT Scallops wih Balsamic Vinegar Dressing

ABOUT 5 NEW POTATOES

SALT AND PEPPER

1 POUND FIRM WHITE FISH FILLET, SUCH AS COD, HADDOCK, OR MONKFISH

2 TABLESPOONS WHITE WINE VINEGAR

6 TABLESPOONS LIGHT EXTRA VIRGIN OLIVE OIL

1 MILD RED OR WHITE ONION, FINELY CHOPPED

2 TABLESPOONS CAPERS

1 LARGE BUNCH (1/2 CUP) CILANTRO, CHOPPED

MOROCCAN FISH SALAD

SERVES 4

Boil the potatoes in lightly salted water until tender, then drain, peel, and cut into 1-inch pieces.

Poach the fish in boiling salted water for 5 minutes or until it just begins to flake when you cut it with a pointed knife. Let it cool and flake it into equal pieces.

Whisk the vinegar and oil together with a little salt and pepper to taste and pour over the fish and potatoes in a serving bowl. Add the rest of the ingredients and mix gently. Serve hot or at room temperature.

1 1/4 CUPS LONG-GRAIN RICE

SALT

4 TO 6 TABLESPOONS MILD EXTRA
VIRGIN OLIVE OIL

JUICE OF 1 LEMON, TO TASTE

PEPPER

5 SCALLIONS, FINELY CHOPPED

1 LARGE BUNCH (1/2 CUP) FLAT-
LEAF PARSLEY OR A MIXTURE OF
HERBS SUCH AS CHIVES, MINT, AND
CILANTRO, CHOPPED

ABOUT 1 POUND CHILLED POACHED
FISH OR SEAFOOD SUCH AS WHITE
FISH, SQUID, SHRIMP, AND MUSSELS

VARIATION

A spectacular version can
be a ring of cold Tomato
Risotto (see page 87) filled
with a variety of poached
seafood dressed with Oil
and Lemon Dressing (see
page 144) or with (cold)
Lemon and Tomato
Dressing (see page 144).
The seafood salad can be
accompanied with simply
cooked navy beans.

SEAFOOD AND RICE SALAD

**Made in large quantities, this is an ideal dish for a
party. It is relatively cheap, beautiful to look at,
can be prepared in advance, and tastes delicious. You
may wish to accompany with Mayonnaise or Aïoli
(see page 220) but it is not essential. The seafood may
include a firm-fleshed white fish, cut into pieces
and poached; squid cut into rings and poached; peeled
cooked shrimp; and mussels, in or out of their shells.
(For preparing mussels and squid see page 216.)**

SERVES 4

Cook the rice in boiling salted water for about 18
minutes, until just tender, then drain. Dress the rice with
the oil, lemon juice, and salt and pepper to taste. Let it
cool and mix with the scallions and parsley. Fold in the
poached seafood.

Serve cold.

FOR THE SOAKED BREAD BASE

4 SLICES COUNTRY BREAD (¹/2-INCH THICK)

³/4 CUP TOMATO JUICE

5 TABLESPOONS OLIVE OIL

2 TABLESPOONS RED OR WHITE WINE VINEGAR

SALT AND PEPPER

¹/2 TO 1 TEASPOON HARISSA (OPTIONAL; SEE PAGE 219)

FOR THE SALAD

2 GREEN OR RED BELL PEPPERS

3 MEDIUM, RIPE TOMATOES

1 (7-OUNCE) CAN TUNA, DRAINED AND FLAKED

3 HARD-BOILED EGGS, QUARTERED

4 TO 8 BLACK OLIVES

1 TO 2 TABLESPOONS CAPERS, SQUEEZED OF THEIR VINEGAR (OPTIONAL)

1 (50-GRAM) CAN ANCHOVIES, DRAINED (OPTIONAL)

3 TO 4 TABLESPOONS EXTRA VIRGIN OLIVE OIL

JUICE OF ¹/2 LEMON

SALT AND PEPPER

ROAST PEPPER, TOMATO, TUNA, AND BREAD SALAD

Tunisia's famous salad *meshweya* ('grilled') becomes a hearty summer's day meal when it is served on a bed of bread soaked with tomato juice and vinaigrette. Use a white rustic or country loaf. Adding Harissa is traditional, but I prefer this simple dish without the complex spice blend.

SERVES 4

Cut the crusts off the bread and toast it. Arrange the slices side by side in a 9-inch-wide shallow bowl.

Mix the tomato juice, olive oil, vinegar, salt and pepper to taste, and Harissa, if using, and pour over the bread so that it is thoroughly soaked.

To make the salad topping, place the peppers and tomatoes on a baking sheet under the broiler, turning them occasionally, or grill them on the barbecue.

Take the tomatoes out as soon as their skins come off easily. Peel and cut them into quarters. Take the peppers out when their skin is blackened in parts and blistered. Skin them, following the directions given on page 216, and cut them into ribbons about ¹/2 inch wide.

Arrange the salad—peppers, tomatoes, flaked tuna, eggs, olives, capers, and anchovies—on the soaked bread in a decorative way.

Mix the oil, lemon juice, and salt and pepper to taste and drizzle over the salad; serve.

1 (750-ML) BOTTLE DRY WHITE WINE

2 1/2 PINTS FISH STOCK OR WATER

2 FRESH RED CHILIES, SEEDED

5 CLOVES GARLIC, SLIVERED

2 POUNDS NEW POTATOES

2 POUNDS PLUM TOMATOES, PEELED AND CUT IN HALF, OR 2 (14-OUNCE) CANS PEELED PLUM TOMATOES

4 BAY LEAVES

A FEW PARSLEY SPRIGS

SALT TO TASTE

5 TABLESPOONS OLIVE OIL

3 TO 4 1/2 POUNDS FISH FILLETS

1 POUND SHELLED SHRIMP (OPTIONAL)

6 SCALLOPS (OPTIONAL)

2 POUNDS MUSSELS, CLEANED AND STEAMED OPEN (SEE PAGE 216; OPTIONAL)

ITALIAN FISH SOUP

This is a dish for a party. I have made it with whole fish—bream, gurnard, red snapper, whiting, and red mullet—which looks dramatic but is difficult to serve and there is the problem of bones to deal with. It is far easier to use fish fillets such as monkfish, cod, turbot, and red mullet. You can make it with fish alone or you may add shrimp and scallops or mussels.

SERVES 6 TO 8

Put the wine and fish stock in a large pan. Add the chilies, garlic, potatoes, tomatoes, bay leaves, parsley, and salt and bring to a boil over medium heat. Simmer for 20 minutes.

Add the oil and the fish fillets and cook for 5 to 10 minutes until they just begin to flake when you cut into them with a pointed knife. Add the shrimp, scallops, and the mussels in their shells, if using, to heat through.

Serve in soup bowls with toasted bread rubbed with garlic. You may put the bread at the bottom of each soup bowl to soak up the broth.

ABOUT 2 LARGE POTATOES, CUT
INTO THICK SLICES

2 MEDIUM TOMATOES, PEELED AND
QUARTERED

1/2 TEASPOON PAPRIKA

1/4 TEASPOON HARISSA (SEE PAGE
216), OR MORE TO TASTE, OR 1
LARGE PINCH CHILI PEPPER

1/2 TEASPOON CUMIN

3 CLOVES GARLIC, CHOPPED

JUICE OF 1/2 LEMON

SALT TO TASTE

3 TABLESPOONS EXTRA VIRGIN
OLIVE OIL

1 POUND WHITE FISH FILLETS,
SKINNED

1 LARGE BUNCH (1/2 CUP) FLAT-
LEAF PARSLEY OR CILANTRO, FINELY
CHOPPED

3 TO 4 SPRIGS MINT, FINELY
CHOPPED

TUNISIAN FISH SOUP
WITH POTATOES

There are fish soups with potatoes
and tomatoes in all the countries around the
Mediterranean. What is different in each
area is the type of fish used and the aromatics.
This simple version is a meal in itself.
Its appeal is the herby and peppery aromatics.
Start with only a little Harissa or chili
pepper and add more later, if you wish. I prefer it not
too peppery. Hake is often used in Tunisia for
this soup, but you can use any firm white fish such
as cod, haddock, or turbot.

SERVES 4

Put all the ingredients except the oil, fish, and herbs together in a pan with 4½ cups water. Simmer for 25 minutes or until the potatoes are tender.

Stir in the oil and add the fish. Cook for 10 minutes more; gently break up the fillets into smaller pieces and add the herbs.

Serve hot with toasted bread.

2 TABLESPOONS BUTTER

1 TABLESPOON SUNFLOWER OR
LIGHT VEGETABLE OIL

1 MEDIUM ONION, CHOPPED

3 CLOVES GARLIC, FINELY CHOPPED

1 MEDIUM LEEK, SLICED

1 CELERY RIB, SLICED

1 CUP DRY WHITE WINE

SALT AND FRESHLY GROUND WHITE
PEPPER

3-INCH STRIP ORANGE PEEL

1 LARGE POTATO, CUT INTO CUBES

1/2 TEASPOON SAFFRON THREADS

1 1/4 POUNDS SKINNED FISH FILLET

2/3 CUP HEAVY CREAM

FISH SOUP WITH SAFFRON AND CREAM

This delicate, creamy soup with the flavors of the south of France is one of our family favorites. It is extremely easy to make with boneless fish fillets such as cod, haddock, whiting, or other white (not oily) fish, or with a mixture of fish and cooked shrimp. Serve it with warmed or slightly toasted bread.

SERVES 4

Heat the butter and oil in a large saucepan over medium heat. Add the onion, garlic, leek, and celery and sauté until they are soft and beginning to color slightly.

Pour in the wine and 2¼ cups water. Season with a little salt and white pepper to taste and add the orange peel. Simmer for 5 minutes.

Add the potato and cook for 20 minutes, adding water if necessary as the liquid evaporates. Add the saffron and fish and cook for 8 to 10 minutes or until the fish turns opaque. Break the fish into pieces, remove the orange peel, stir in the cream, and cook for 1 to 2 more minutes. Serve hot.

VARIATION

Replace about 7 ounces of the fish with cooked shrimp and add them to the pan just before you add the cream.

DESSERTS

The usual Mediterranean way to end a meal is with fruit: figs, grapes, apricots, dates, melons and watermelons, peaches, plums, cherries, apples, pears, or oranges. Simply bring a bowl to the table, or peel and cut up a selection and arrange it on a platter. Another tradition is to offer dried fruit and nuts with the after-dinner coffee. Most of the desserts in this chapter are made with fruit to celebrate the Mediterranean's rich bounty.

ABOUT 2 POUNDS FRUIT, PEELED IF
NECESSARY

4 TABLESPOONS SUGAR, OR TO
TASTE

JUICE OF ½ TO 1 LEMON

MACERATED FRUIT SALAD

**Leaving the fruit to macerate in a
mixture of lemon and sugar releases their
juices and gives them a richer, more
intense flavor. Use a good variety of fruit
such as bananas, oranges, apples,
pears, apricots, strawberries, raspberries,
blueberries, seedless grapes,
kiwis, cherries, mangoes, and pineapple.**

SERVES 4

VARIATION

Instead of lemon juice,
sprinkle with 4 tablespoons
cognac or kirsch.

Cut the fruit into pieces or leave them whole if small.
Layer in a large bowl, sprinkling each layer with sugar
and lemon juice, and let the fruit macerate for at least
an hour.

2 POUNDS UNPEELED ORANGES,
CUT INTO ¼-INCH SLICES

2½ CUPS SUGAR

ORANGE SLICES IN SYRUP

**This preserve makes a ready sweet to serve with a
dollop of thick heavy cream.**

SERVES 8 TO 12

VARIATION

If you want it to keep for
several months, use twice
the amount of sugar.

Put layers of orange slices and sugar in a pan. Cover
with water and simmer gently over medium heat for 1½
hours, adding water to keep the fruit covered.

When cool enough to handle, press the orange
slices into a jar and cover with syrup. Store in the
refrigerator (it will keep well for weeks).

2 POUNDS FRUIT—CHOOSE 2 OR
MORE FROM THE FOLLOWING:
APPLES, PEARS, PEACHES, PLUMS,
GREENGAGES, APRICOTS,
GOOSEBERRIES, CHERRIES, AND
GRAPES

1¹/₄ CUPS SUGAR

FRUIT COMPOTES

**Fresh fruits poached in sugar syrup make
an easy sweet. For a more glamorous
dessert they can be served on a bed of Rice
Pudding (see page 198) or on an Almond Custard
(see page 201).**

SERVES 4

To prepare the fruit, wash it and peel, halve, and stone
it if necessary. Apples and pears should be peeled, cored,
and sliced.

To make the syrup, bring 2 cups water to a boil with
the sugar over medium heat. The sweetness of the syrup
is a matter of personal taste and the tartness of the
particular fruit.

Put the fruit in the boiling syrup. Each fruit needs
a different cooking time, which also depends on their
degree of ripeness. Ripe fresh fruit should be poached
very briefly. Cherries, gooseberries, and grapes need only
1 to 3 minutes, apricots and plums require 5 minutes;
peaches 10; apple slices 10 to 15; clementines with their
peels (cut in half) may need 25 minutes; and pears, if
they are unripe and hard, need more than 40 minutes.
Orange slices and tangerines can be cooked for 1 hour.
For mixed compotes it is best to poach the fruits
separately or to add them at different times so that none
is overcooked. Serve at room temperature or chilled.

VARIATIONS

As special flavoring you can
add to the syrup the peel of
a lemon or an orange, the
juice of ½ lemon, a stick of
cinnamon, a few cloves, or
a vanilla pod or a few drops
of vanilla extract.

At the end, add a few
tablespoons of kirsch,
cognac, or Cointreau.

Instead of water, you could
use a mixture of red or
white wine and water.

*OVERLEAF From left to right:
Cherry, Grape, and Apricot Compotes*

2 LARGE QUINCES

1 1/4 CUPS SUGAR

2/3 CUP CLOTTED OR THICK HEAVY CREAM

STEWED QUINCE

You will find this all over the Mediterranean, but in Turkey it is the most popular dessert. It is one of my favorites.

SERVES 4

Cut the quinces in half through the core. They are very hard and you need a strong knife and strong pressure to cut them. Trim the blackened ends, but leave the cores and seeds—they will provide a lovely jelly.

In a wide shallow pan over medium heat, put the sugar and 3½ cups water (there should be enough to cover the quinces in one layer) and bring to a boil. Put in the fruit, cut side down, and simmer, covered, until it feels tender when you pierce it with the point of a knife. The cooking time can vary between 20 minutes to 1 hour depending on the quality and ripeness of the fruit.

Lift out the fruit and place it on a dish. When it is cool enough to handle, cut out the cores carefully and return the cores to the pan with the syrup. Boil the syrup, uncovered, until it is thick enough to coat the back of a spoon—it turns a rich garnet red.

Return the fruit to the pan, cut side down, and cook in the syrup for 10 minutes.

Arrange in a serving dish, cut side up, with the syrup poured over. Serve with a dollop of cream in the center, or pass the cream for people to help themselves.

1 1/4 CUPS SUGAR

1/4 TEASPOON GROUND GINGER

A FEW DROPS VANILLA EXTRACT

4 LARGE YELLOW PEACHES

PEACHES IN
A FRAGRANT SYRUP

**These peaches are not too sweet; they have a
very delicate vanilla and ginger flavor.
There must be enough syrup to cover them and it
can be reused to make another batch
if necessary. Use large yellow peaches that are
firm and not too ripe.**

SERVES 4

For the syrup, boil 4 1/2 cups water and the sugar until the sugar is dissolved. Add the ginger and vanilla extract and remove from the heat.

To peel the peaches, drop them in boiling water (off the heat) and leave in the water for a few minutes. Drain the peaches and slip the skins off. Poach the peaches, whole, in the syrup for 15 to 20 minutes, until very tender. Leave them in the syrup until you are ready to serve. Serve chilled or at room temperature, without the syrup.

Serve with Almond Custard (page 201) flavored with a sweet wine such as Beaume de Vin de Pêches or cassis, or with Honey Ice Cream (see page 202).

8 PEACHES, CUT IN HALF, UNPEELED, STONES REMOVED

$1/2$ CUP AMARETTO OR MARSALA

2 TO 3 DROPS VANILLA EXTRACT

4 TABLESPOONS SUGAR, OR TO TASTE

ROASTED PEACHES

This very simple and delicious way of preparing peaches is from southern Italy.

SERVES 4

Preheat the oven to 375° F.

Arrange the peaches in a shallow baking dish, cut side up. Mix the Amaretto with the vanilla and 2 tablespoons of the sugar, and pour over the peaches, so that a little settles in the hollows.

Bake for 10 to 20 minutes or until soft (the time varies, depending on the size and ripeness of the fruit).

Sprinkle the tops with the remaining sugar and put under the broiler until caramelized. The baking can be done in advance, but the last step must be carried out just before serving. Serve hot.

FOR THE RICE PUDDING

1 CUP ARBORIO OR PUDDING RICE

4 1/2 CUPS MILK

3/4 CUP SUGAR, OR TO TASTE

2 TABLESPOONS ROSE WATER

1/2 TEASPOON GROUND MASTIC

FOR THE FRUITS POACHED IN SYRUP

1 1/4 CUP SUGAR

JUICE OF 1/4 LEMON

3 PEACHES OR NECTARINES, PEELED AND QUARTERED

3 PEARS, PEELED AND QUARTERED

6 APRICOTS, PITTED AND CUT IN HALF

VARIATION

Add 1 teaspoon ground cardamom with the milk and omit the mastic.

POACHED FRUIT WITH RICE PUDDING

**Mastic and rose water—two Arab flavorings—
give the rice pudding a delicious exotic
flavor that marries well with the stewed fruit topping.
Mastic is a resin from a tree, and can be
bought in small grains or crystals in Greek and
Middle Eastern stores. You have to pound
it yourself to a powder, with a little sugar, with a
pestle and mortar. You must use very little
because too much can be unpleasant. An alternative
to mastic is ground cardamom (see Variation),
which is easy to obtain and easier to use.**

SERVES 6

To make the rice pudding, put the rice in a large pan with 1 1/2 cups water over medium heat. Bring to a boil, then simmer for 8 minutes or until the water is absorbed. Add the milk and simmer over very low heat, stirring occasionally, for 30 to 45 minutes until the rice is very soft and the milk is almost, but not entirely, absorbed. Add the sugar and stir until dissolved. Add the rose water and the mastic and stir vigorously. Pour into a shallow serving dish.

To poach the fruit, put the sugar, 1 cup water, and the lemon juice in a pan over medium heat, bring to a boil, then simmer gently.

Meanwhile, pour boiling water over the peaches or nectarines to loosen their skins, then peel them.

Put the different fruits in the syrup separately, in batches, because they cook at different rates. The time also depends on their size and degree of ripeness. Peaches and apricots can take 6 minutes only, and pears much longer. Turn the fruit pieces over once if they are not entirely covered by the syrup.

As they become tender, lift them out of the syrup onto a plate, to drain the excess syrup. Let cool to room temperature and arrange them in a flower pattern on top of the rice pudding to serve.

1 POUND BLACK CHERRIES

3 EGGS

1/2 CUP SUPERFINE SUGAR

1 TABLESPOON ALL-PURPOSE FLOUR

2 DROPS VANILLA EXTRACT

2 TABLESPOONS CALVADOS OR KIRSCH

2/3 CUP HEAVY CREAM

1/2 CUP MILK

POWDERED SUGAR

CHERRY CLAFOUTIS

This old Provençal country dish of cherries baked in custard remains popular. There is no need to pit the cherries, but you can do so if you prefer.

SERVES 4

Preheat the oven to 350° F.

Wash and dry the cherries. Butter a shallow 8½-inch baking dish and put in the cherries.

Beat the eggs together with the sugar and flour. Add the vanilla and Calvados or kirsch, and gradually beat in the cream and milk.

Pour the mixture over the cherries and bake for about 45 minutes or until the cream sets and a light golden crust forms.

Serve warm, sprinkled with powdered sugar. You may put it under the broiler for 1 minute to caramelize the sugar.

SAUTÉED FRUIT WITH ALMOND CUSTARD

FOR THE SAUTÉED FRUIT

6 TABLESPOONS UNSALTED BUTTER

3 APPLES, PEELED AND CUT INTO SMALL PIECES

2 PEARS, PEELED AND CUT INTO SMALL PIECES

6 APRICOTS, PITTED AND CUT INTO PIECES

1 DOZEN OR MORE CHERRIES

3 TO 4 TABLESPOONS SUGAR, OR TO TASTE

3 TABLESPOONS CALVADOS OR ARMAGNAC

FOR THE ALMOND CUSTARD

3/4 CUP SUGAR

5 EGG YOLKS

1/2 CUP ALL-PURPOSE FLOUR

2 1/4 CUPS MILK

2 TO 3 TABLESPOONS KIRSCH, RUM, CALVADOS, OR ARMAGNAC

1 CUP BLANCHED GROUND ALMONDS

3 DROPS ALMOND OR VANILLA EXTRACT (OPTIONAL)

One of my favorite summer desserts is an assortment of poached Fruit (see page 198) on an almond custard, served chilled. In the winter, sautéed fruit on steaming hot custard is an irresistible sweet. All kinds of fruit can be sautéed. Grinding blanched almonds yourself in a food processor will give a better texture than using bought ground almonds. The almond extract is optional; in the past, the almond flavor was intensified by adding a few bitter almonds.

SERVES 6

To prepare the fruit, melt the butter in a large skillet over medium heat and sauté the apples and pears, stirring and turning them over occasionally, for 15 minutes, or until they are tender. Add the apricots and cherries and sauté briefly, until soft. Add the sugar and alcohol and cook for a few more minutes. Remove from the heat and set aside.

To make the custard, beat the sugar with the egg yolks to a light pale cream, then beat in the flour.

Bring the milk to a boil in a heavy-bottomed pan. Very gradually pour the milk into the egg mixture, beating vigorously until well blended, then pour the mixture back into the pan.

Cook over very low heat until the mixture thickens, stirring constantly so that lumps do not form and the cream does not stick to the bottom. If the cream does

VARIATIONS

Serve the almond custard cold topped with chilled poached fruit.

Serve cold almond custard as a bed for raw fruit such as strawberries, raspberries, blueberries, white and black grapes, pitted fresh dates, sliced kiwi, and orange slices cut into small pieces.

2 1/4 CUPS MILK

4 EGG YOLKS

5 OUNCES LAVENDER, ACCACIA, OR OTHER CLEAR, PERFUMED HONEY

2/3 CUP HEAVY CREAM

1 TABLESPOON ORANGE-FLOWER WATER

burn slightly, be careful not to scrape the burned bits into the custard.

Stir in the alcohol, almonds, and the almond or vanilla extract if using, being careful to add only a few drops of almond extract, as too much tastes unpleasant. Cook for a few more moments.

Pour the custard into a wide shallow serving dish and spoon the fruit with their juices over the top.

If you want to prepare the custard in advance, put the custard in a baking dish and heat it through in the oven when ready to serve, then spoon the hot fruit on top.

HONEY ICE CREAM

This fragrant ice cream is a specialty of Provence where it is made with lavender honey.

SERVES 6

In a saucepan, bring the milk to a boil and remove from the heat. Beat the egg yolks to a pale cream color, then beat in the honey, cream, and finally, the hot milk.

Return the mixture to the pan and stir with a wooden spoon over low heat until it thickens to a light cream, but do not let it boil or it will curdle. Stir in the orange-flower water.

Let it cool to room temperature and pour into a serving bowl. Cover with plastic wrap and freeze overnight or at least 5 hours before serving. You may serve straight from the freezer.

ABOUT *1 CUP SUGAR*

JUICE OF 1 LEMON

5 PEARS, PEELED AND CORED

POIRE WILLIAM LIQUEUR OR A FRUIT BRANDY (OPTIONAL)

PEAR GRANITA

SERVES *4 TO 6*

In a wide pan that can hold the pears in one layer, boil 1 cup water and the sugar with the lemon juice until the sugar dissolves. Add more sugar, if necessary, at the end, depending on the sweetness of the pears.

Put in the pears and simmer over medium heat, covered, for 10 minutes or until they are soft.

Purée the pears with their syrup in a food processor. Taste for sugar and add more if necessary. Pour into ice cube trays, cover with plastic wrap, and place in the freezer overnight.

Put the frozen cubes, in batches, in the food processor and process to a very fine, frothy slush. Pour into a serving bowl and serve at once or return to the freezer, covered with plastic wrap.

Take out 10 minutes before you are ready to serve. If you like, pass around the pear liqueur or fruit brandy for people to help themselves to a drizzle.

1 CUP SUGAR

JUICE OF $^{1}/_{2}$ LEMON

2 POUNDS RIPE APRICOTS, PITTED

KIRSCH OR FRUIT BRANDY (OPTIONAL)

APRICOT GRANITA

This water ice has a refreshingly tart flavor.

SERVES 4 TO 6

Boil 1 cup water and the sugar with the lemon juice in a wide pan until the sugar dissolves.

Put in the apricots and simmer over medium heat, covered, for 5 minutes or until they are very tender.

Purée the apricots with their syrup in a food processor. Pour into ice cube trays, cover with plastic wrap, and place in the freezer overnight.

Put the frozen cubes, in batches, in the food processor and process to a very fine, frothy slush. Pour into a serving bowl and serve at once or return to the freezer, covered with plastic wrap.

Take out 10 minutes before you are ready to serve. If you like, pass around the kirsch or fruit brandy for people to help themselves to a tablespoon or so.

LEFT Apricot Granita and Pear Granita (page 203)

4 GOLDEN DELICIOUS APPLES,
PEELED, CORED, AND SLICED

2/3 CUP FRUITY DRY WHITE WINE

1/2 CUP SUPERFINE SUGAR

3 EGG YOLKS

3 TABLESPOONS CALVADOS

2/3 CUP HEAVY CREAM

FROZEN APPLE FOOL
WITH CALVADOS

This is called a *parfait* in France.

SERVES 4

Put the apples and the wine in a pan and simmer, covered, for 5 to 10 minutes until the apples are soft. Remove the lid and raise the heat to reduce the liquid.

Add half the sugar, mash the apples with a potato masher or fork, and cook, stirring, until the apple purée is thick and most of the liquid has disappeared. Remove the pan from the heat.

Beat the egg yolks with the remaining sugar until they turn a pale cream color. Pour over the apple purée, stirring vigorously, then place over low heat, stirring constantly, for 30 seconds. Add the Calvados, let the mixture cool to room temperature, and chill in the refrigerator.

Whip the heavy cream to firm peaks and fold it into the cold apple purée. Line a bowl with plastic wrap and pour the mixture into the bowl. Cover the top with plastic wrap and freeze overnight.

To serve, remove the top layer of plastic wrap, turn out onto a serving plate, and remove the remaining plastic wrap.

VARIATIONS

Add 3 drops vanilla extract, a small stick of cinnamon, and 2 cloves to the liquid. Remove the whole spices before mashing the apples.

Pears may be used instead of apples with kirsch or Poire William.

4 EGG YOLKS

3/4 CUP SUPERFINE SUGAR

1 1/4 CUPS LIGHT CREAM

4 TABLESPOONS ARMAGNAC OR
COGNAC

1 1/4 CUPS HEAVY CREAM

7 OUNCES MARRONS GLACÉS,
DICED

SEMI-FREDDO WITH MARRONS GLACÉS

Italian specialty food stores sell broken pieces of marrons glacés, which are much cheaper than the usual product.

SERVES 4 TO 6

Beat the yolks with the sugar until they turn a pale cream color. Bring the light cream to a boil, remove from the heat, and beat it into the egg mixture.

Return the mixture to the pan and cook over low heat, stirring constantly; do not let it boil or it will curdle. Cook until the cream is thick enough to coat the back of a spoon.

Add the Armagnac or cognac to the custard, cover with plastic wrap, let the custard cool to room temperature before putting in the freezer for 1 hour.

Beat the heavy cream until stiff and fold it into the cold custard, then fold in the marrons glacés.

To shape the ice cream into a dome that is easy to unmold, line a bowl with plastic wrap and pour the mixture in, cover with another piece of plastic wrap, and freeze overnight.

To serve, remove the top layer of plastic wrap, and turn out onto a serving plate, and remove the remaining plastic wrap.

7 ounces California pitted prunes

¹/3 cup Armagnac brandy

1 ¹/4 cups whipping cream

2 tablespoons superfine sugar

2 drops vanilla extract

FROZEN CREAM WITH PRUNES AND ARMAGNAC

This light chantilly-type cream with a strong flavor of Armagnac is easy to make and tastes delicious and can be taken out of the freezer just before serving.

SERVES 4

Chop the prunes coarsely in a food processor, add the Armagnac, and soak for 1 hour.

Whip the cream until it forms peaks, then beat in the sugar and vanilla. Fold in the prunes and Armagnac.

Cover with plastic wrap, let cool to room temperature before freezing, and freeze for at least 4 hours. You can serve it straight out of the freezer.

1 1/4 CUPS MEDIUM-GROUND
COUSCOUS

6 TABLESPOONS SUGAR, OR TO
TASTE

2 TABLESPOONS PEANUT OR
SUNFLOWER OIL

3/4 CUP MIXED NUTS SUCH AS
WALNUTS, BLANCHED ALMONDS,
HAZELNUTS, PISTACHIOS, AND PINE
NUTS

4 OUNCES CALIFORNIA DATES,
PITTED AND CUT INTO PIECES

1 1/4 CUPS MILK

SWEET COUSCOUS WITH NUTS AND DATES

Couscous is the Berber food of North Africa. This sweet couscous is more of a breakfast dish or afternoon snack than an after-dinner dessert. It is tasty and satisfying comfort food.

SERVES 4

Preheat the oven to 400° F.

Put the couscous in a round, ovenproof serving dish. Boil 1¼ cups water with 4 tablespoons of the sugar and all of the oil. Pour over the couscous and stir well. Let soak for about 15 minutes, stirring occasionally, until the water has been absorbed.

Rub the grain between your hands to remove any lumps that stick together. Add more sugar to taste.

Toast the nuts very lightly under the broiler or in a dry skillet and chop them coarsely. Stir them into the grain with the dates. Cover the dish with a lid or foil and heat through for 20 minutes in the oven.

Heat the milk and serve the couscous hot, accompanied by the milk and extra sugar for people to help themselves.

¹/2 CUP SOFTENED UNSALTED BUTTER

3 EGGS

³/4 CUP SUPERFINE SUGAR

1 ¹/4 CUPS BLANCHED COARSELY GROUND ALMONDS

2 TO 3 DROPS ALMOND EXTRACT

2 POUNDS APRICOTS, PITTED AND CUT IN HALF

2 TABLESPOONS POWDERED SUGAR

HEAVY CREAM

FOR THE SAUCE

1 CUP SMOOTH APRICOT JAM OR JELLY

1 TO 2 TABLESPOONS KIRSCH OR APRICOT BRANDY

VARIATION

Instead of apricots, use pears, peeled, cored, cut in half, and boiled in water for about 15 minutes or until almost tender.

APRICOT AND ALMOND PUDDING

Apricots give this old Provençal specialty a refreshing tartness.

SERVES 6

Preheat the oven to 350° F.

Blend the butter and eggs with the sugar in a food processor. Add the almonds and almond extract and continue to blend to a soft cream. Pour into a 12-inch baking dish.

Arrange the apricot halves on top, cut side down, pressing them into the butter mixture. Bake for about 45 minutes or until it is firm and lightly colored. Let cool to room temperature.

To make the sauce, heat the jam with 3 tablespoons water and the liqueur, and stir until it melts. Let the sauce cool.

Serve the pudding cold, sprinkled with powdered sugar. Accompany with the sauce and a bowl of cream.

212

1 POUND RICOTTA

3/4 CUP SUPERFINE SUGAR, OR TO
TASTE

5 EGGS, SEPARATED

2 TEASPOONS ORANGE-FLOWER
WATER

GRATED ZEST OF 1/2 LEMON

1/3 CUP DICED CANDIED ORANGE
PEEL

VARIATION

Use a few drops of vanilla
extract or 1½ teaspoons
cinnamon, instead of the
orange-flower water.

RICOTTA CAKE

**This rich Sicilian cake is a bit like a soufflé.
The orange-flower water is a legacy of the old
Arab occupation of the island.**

SERVES 8

Preheat the oven to 350° F.

In a food processor, blend the ricotta, sugar, egg yolks, orange-flower water, and lemon zest to a homogenous cream.

Fold in the diced candied orange peel.

Beat the egg whites stiff and lightly fold them into the ricotta mixture.

Pour into a greased and floured, preferably nonstick 8-inch cake pan and bake for 45 minutes or until brown on top. The cake rises quite high. Let it cool before turning out onto a serving plate.

4 OUNCES BITTERSWEET
CHOCOLATE

4 TABLESPOONS UNSALTED BUTTER

4 EGGS, SEPARATED

1/2 CUP SUPERFINE SUGAR

CHOCOLATE CAKE

**This has such a wonderfully creamy and soft
texture that it is more of a pudding than a cake.**

SERVES 6

Preheat the oven to 300° F.

In the top of a double boiler, melt the chocolate and
butter. Beat the egg yolks and the sugar until they turn a
pale cream color, then beat in the chocolate mixture.

Beat the egg whites until stiff and lightly fold them
into the chocolate and egg mixture.

Pour into a buttered, preferably nonstick 8-inch
cake pan and bake for 30 minutes. Leave it in the oven
for 30 minutes before turning it out onto a serving plate.
Let the cake cool before serving.

4 1/2 CUPS BLANCHED GROUND
ALMONDS

1 CUP SUPERFINE SUGAR

1 1/2 TEASPOONS CINNAMON

3 DROPS (NO MORE) ALMOND
EXTRACT (OPTIONAL)

2 TABLESPOONS ORANGE-FLOWER
WATER

4 EGG YOLKS

5 SHEETS PHYLLO DOUGH

3 TO 4 TABLESPOONS UNSALTED
BUTTER, MELTED, OR SUNFLOWER
OIL

POWDERED SUGAR

MOROCCAN ALMOND 'SNAKE'

**This is a good pastry to make for a party.
It is very rich and you serve small pieces. It takes
its Moroccan name *m'hencha* from the word *hencha*,
meaning snake, because it looks like a curled snake.**

SERVES 12

Preheat the oven to 350° F.

In a bowl, mix the almonds, sugar, 1/2 teaspoon of
the cinnamon, and the almond extract if using. Add the

orange-flower water and 3 egg yolks, and combine well with your hands.

Open the packet of phyllo only when you are ready to use the pastry. Take 5 sheets out and keep them in a pile. Brush the top sheet lightly with melted butter.

Form one-fifth of the almond paste into a long, thin sausage the thickness of your thumb, and place it along one long edge of the phyllo sheet, about ¾ inch from the end. Lift the edge of the top sheet up over the paste and roll up into a loose, long, thin roll. To curve this roll without tearing the pastry, first wrinkle the pastry by pushing both ends of the roll gently toward the middle. Grease a flat ovenproof dish or line a baking sheet with foil. Lift the pastry roll carefully onto the middle of the dish and curve it gently into a snail shape.

Repeat with the remaining filling and sheets of phyllo, placing the long, wrinkled rolls end to end, to make a long coil. Mix the remaining egg yolk with 1 teaspoon water, brush the top of the roll, and bake for 45 minutes until crisp and browned on top.

Let cool to room temperature and serve, dusted with powdered sugar and the remaining cinnamon.

BASICS

PREPARATIONS

TO CLEAN AND PREPARE SQUID

Pull the head away from the body pouch and discard the soft innards that come out with it. Discard the insides of the pouch—the inkbag, if any, and the icicle-shaped transparent cuttlebone. Keep the tentacles in their bunches but discard the eyes and the small round cartilage at the base of the tentacles by cutting with a sharp knife just above the eyes (be careful that ink doesn't squirt out at you from the eyes). Rinse thoroughly. Cut the body into rings.

TO CLEAN AND PREPARE MUSSELS

Scrub the mussels, pull off the beards, and wash in several changes of cold water. Test to see if they are alive: discard any that are broken and those that are too heavy or too light, or do not close when they are tapped or dipped in cold water. To steam them open, put them in a large pan with a finger of water and the lid on. Take off the heat as soon as they open (in about 1 minute). Discard any that remain closed.

TO ROAST AND PEEL BELL PEPPERS

Many dishes call for roasted red bell peppers. Choose fleshy peppers. Put them on an oven tray under the broiler, about $3\frac{1}{2}$ inches from the flame, or grill them on a barbecue. Turn them until their skins are black and blistered all over.

An easier method is to roast them in a 350° F. oven for 1 hour (or a very hot oven for 30 minutes) until they are soft and their skins begin to blister and blacken. Turn them once during the roasting. To loosen the skins, put the peppers in a pan with a tight-fitting lid or in a heavy-duty plastic bag and twist it closed. Let steam for 10 to 15 minutes to loosen the skins.

When the peppers are cool enough to handle, peel them and remove the stems and seeds. Reserve the juice that comes out, and strain it to remove the seeds. The juice can be used as part of a dressing.

Roast peppers can be kept, covered with oil, for several months. Store them in a cool, dark place or in the refrigerator.

To Broil or Roast Eggplant Slices

These days many people prefer broiled or roasted eggplants to fried ones, but very often they are not cooked enough.

Cut the eggplants into ¼- to ⅓-inch slices, lengthwise or into rounds, sprinkle with salt, and let them drain to degorge their juices. Rinse and dry them. (This process can be omitted—it is not always necessary with smaller eggplants.) Brush both sides with oil and place under the broiler or over a charcoal fire, turning to brown both sides.

Alternatively, place the slices on a baking sheet and bake in a very hot oven until tender and lightly browned.

To Prepare Hearts of Small Globe Artichokes

With a small sharp knife, cut off the stem and cut away or pull off the tough outer leaves, starting at the base, until you are left with the pale inner leaves. Slice off the tough ends of these, open the center and scoop out the prickly inner choke with a pointed spoon.

To Prepare Bottoms of Large Globe Artichokes

Cut away all the leaves to the bare flat bottom with a sharp pointed knife, then cut or scrape away the choke from the center.

RECIPES

SALT AND PEPPER TO TASTE

1 TABLESPOON WHITE WINE VINEGAR OR LEMON JUICE

3¹/2 TABLESPOONS MILD EXTRA VIRGIN OLIVE OIL

VINAIGRETTE

In the Mediterranean lemon juice is often used in a salad dressing instead of vinegar.

Stir the salt and pepper into the vinegar until the salt is dissolved, then whisk in the oil.

1 TO 2 CLOVES GARLIC, FINELY CHOPPED OR CRUSHED

2 TO 3 TABLESPOONS EXTRA VIRGIN OLIVE OIL

8 RIPE PLUM TOMATOES, PEELED AND CHOPPED

SALT AND PEPPER

1 TO 2 TEASPOONS SUGAR

FRESH TOMATO SAUCE

This sauce can be used for many dishes including sautéed fish and pasta.

MAKES ENOUGH TO SERVE 4 TO 6

Sauté the garlic in the oil over medium-low heat until the aroma rises. Add the tomatoes, salt and pepper, and sugar and simmer for 10 to 15 minutes to reduce slightly.

VARIATIONS

Add 3 tablespoons chopped parsley or basil.

Add 1 tablespoon freshly grated ginger or the juice of a 1-inch piece of ginger, peeled and crushed in a garlic press.

A Moroccan version uses ¹/2 teaspoon powdered ginger, ¹/4 teaspoon saffron, and ¹/4 teaspoon chili pepper. It is sometimes garnished with 6 or 7 olives and ¹/2 Preserved Lemon Peel, chopped (see page 219).

PRESERVED LEMON PEEL

Wash the lemons and make two vertical cuts in a cross, almost but not quite through the lemons, so that the sections still hold together at the stem.

Sprinkle about ½ cup plus 2 tablespoons salt for about 8 lemons inside on the cut flesh, then close them and pack them tightly in a clean jar. Squeeze enough fresh lemon juice over them to cover. The salt will draw out the juices and the peel will soften within a week. They will be ready to use in 3 to 4 weeks.

Rinse off the salt before using and discard the flesh. It is the peel alone that you want.

2 OUNCES DRIED HOT RED CHILI PEPPERS, STEMS AND SEEDS REMOVED

4 CLOVES GARLIC, PEELED

1 TEASPOON GROUND CARAWAY

1 TEASPOON GROUND CORIANDER

ABOUT ½ TEASPOON SALT

EXTRA VIRGIN OLIVE OIL

HARISSA

**This hot chili paste is used in many
North African dishes.**

MAKES ABOUT 1 CUP

Soak the chili peppers in water for 30 minutes until soft. Drain and pound with the garlic, spices, and a little salt with a pestle and mortar, or blend in a food processor, adding just enough oil, by the tablespoon, to make a soft paste. Press into a jar and cover with a thin layer of oil. This way it keeps very well in the refrigerator for several weeks.

1 EGG YOLK

JUICE OF ½ TO 1 LEMON

½ TEASPOON SALT

1¼ CUPS OIL—A MIXTURE OF
SUNFLOWER OR LIGHT VEGETABLE
OIL WITH EXTRA VIRGIN OLIVE OIL

4 CLOVES GARLIC, OR MORE TO
TASTE, CRUSHED IN A PRESS OR
POUNDED TO A PASTE (IF YOU ARE
MAKING AÏOLI)

MAYONNAISE AND AÏOLI

**Aïoli is the garlic mayonnaise common to
Spain and southern France. It is made in the same
way as mayonnaise but with garlic added.
It is used as a dip for crudités, and with boiled
vegetables or fish and seafood.
It is best not to use olive oil alone, as the
result is too strong and overpowering. Instead,
use a mixture of a bland vegetable oil with
olive oil: the proportion may vary. I like to use
⅔ vegetable oil and ⅓ olive oil. It is usual to
beat the garlic with the egg yolk first until it is a
pale cream color, but you may prefer to add it
at the end when you can taste and decide how much
you want to use.
To ensure success, all the ingredients must be at
room temperature (do not use an egg straight from
the refrigerator) and the bowl should be warm.**

MAKES 1¾ CUPS

VARIATION

For a rouille, which goes
very well with fish soup,
add 1 to 2 teaspoons
paprika and a large pinch
of cayenne.

Put the egg yolk in a warmed bowl and place the bowl on a damp cloth to prevent it from slipping. Add some of the lemon juice and a little salt.

Add the oil, a little at a time—first drop by drop, then in a thin stream—vigorously beating constantly with a hand-held beater.

As the oil becomes absorbed and the sauce emulsifies, it will thicken to a heavy consistency.

Finally, beat in the garlic and the rest of the lemon juice to taste.

1 TABLESPOON ACTIVE DRY YEAST

A PINCH SUGAR

SCANT 2 CUPS LUKEWARM WATER

5¼ CUPS WHITE UNBLEACHED HARD WHEAT FLOUR

2 TEASPOONS SALT

5 TABLESPOONS EXTRA VIRGIN OLIVE OIL (PLUS A LITTLE TO OIL THE DOUGH AND PAN)

FOCACCIA

Flatbreads are very common in the Mediterranean region. They are usually quite soft, often flavored with herbs or spices, and sometimes embellished with ingredients such as chopped olives, fried onions, and tomatoes. In the Arab world they can be sprinkled with sesame, fennel, caraway, anise, or onion seed. My favorite for making at home is the versatile Italian focaccia. This recipe is for basic focaccia. Several variations follow.

SERVES 6 TO 8

Preheat the oven to 425° F. for at least 30 minutes. If you have a baking stone, put it in the oven.

Dissolve the yeast and sugar in about half the warm water and set aside for 10 minutes until it froths.

Put the flour and salt in a large bowl, and make a well in the center. Pour in the yeast mixture and 3 tablespoons of the oil and mix with a wooden spoon.

Add the remaining warm water very gradually—just enough to make a soft ball that holds together, mixing first with the wooden spoon, then working it in with your hand to incorporate the flour.

Turn onto a lightly floured surface and knead for about 10 minutes until very smooth and elastic, adding a little flour if too sticky, or a drop of water if too dry.

Pour a little oil in the bowl and turn the dough in it to grease it all over. Cover the bowl with plastic wrap and set aside to rise in a warm place for about 1½ hours or until doubled in size.

Punch the dough down and knead very briefly to punch out the air, then use your oiled fingertips to press the dough into the bottom of 1 or 2 oiled baking sheets. (I use 2 round 11-inch pans, but a large rectangular one will do very well.) As the dough is very elastic and springs back, you may need to stretch it again a few times. A focaccia can be thick or thin, and the flattened dough can be ¼- to ½-inch thick. Cover with a towel or foil and let rise again in a warm place for about 45 minutes.

Just before baking, make many deep holes all over the dough with your finger, and sprinkle or brush all over with the remaining olive oil.

Place the focaccias one at a time into the oven and bake for 30 minutes or until the crusts are crisp and golden. Turn out and place on a rack. Focaccia can be served at room temperature but is best eaten hot or warm, cut into squares, rectangles, or wedges. You may also freeze the focaccia for up to 1 year.

VARIATIONS

Before baking:

Sprinkle 1½ teaspoons coarse sea salt over the top.

Sprinkle with 2 to 3 chopped cloves garlic and the leaves of 2 sprigs rosemary or 2 tablespoons chopped sage leaves.

Sprinkle with 1 tablespoon chopped oregano and 18 black olives, pitted and finely chopped.

Spread with Fresh Tomato Sauce (see page 218), reduced until the liquid has disappeared, and sprinkle with 1 tablespoon chopped oregano, 3 chopped cloves garlic, and 8 pitted and halved black olives.

Brush with a mixture of 3 tablespoons anchovy paste (or olive paste) and 2 tablespoons olive oil.

Top with 2 large onions, sliced and fried in 3 tablespoons extra virgin olive oil over very low heat for about 45 minutes until very soft. Cover the pan for the first 25 minutes, and stir occasionally. You may also let the onions brown and caramelize.

Roast and peel 3 red bell peppers (see page 216); cut them into ribbons and scatter over the dough with 3 chopped cloves garlic.

INDEX

Page numbers in *italics* refer
to illustrations